At the Top of the Stairs

The Story of Leeds Central, Northern Soul and Jazz Funk

By

Steve Taylor

Grosvenor House
Publishing Limited

This book is published by
Grosvenor House Publishing Ltd
Link House
140 The Broadway, Tolworth, Surrey, KT6 7HT.
www.grosvenorhousepublishing.co.uk

A CIP record for this book
is available from the British Library

ISBN 978-1-83975-574-3

This book is dedicated to my wife, Jill, daughters Ella and Robyn, and granddaughters Aaliyah and Eva, to give them some insight into my youth, and also to provide an explanation why I've got so many records.

SPECIAL THANKS TO THE FOLLOWING, WHOSE STORIES FORM THE CRUX OF THE BOOK.

Chris Mallows

Dave Raby

David Okonofua

Derek T Barnett

Denis Billingham

Gary Davison

Gip Damone

Glen Campbell

Hunter Smith

Ian Dewhirst

Jane Barber

Jeff Leighton

Jill Taylor

Keith Atkinson

Lee Ingham

Malc Burton

Mally Meah

Michelle Dudhill

Mike Eastwood

Pat Brady

Paul Rowan

Paul Schofield

Pete Dillon

Richard Minott

Richard Searling

Rick Cooper

Simon Andrews

Steve Caesar

Steve Cook

Steve Luigi

Steve Walwyn

Swish

Twink

Vince Enyori

CONTENTS

❀

PREFACE

❀

I am not a writer, as you'll soon discover. I am a 61-year-old Loiner, Soul fan and businessman, who spent his youth on the Northern Soul and Jazz Funk scenes, and to this day frequents Northern Soul and Modern Soul venues, with a particular love of Janet Crowe and Colin Curtis's events, and Richard Searling events, particularly the Blackpool International Soul Festival.

I have spent most of my business life trying to condense thoughts and communication into simple bullet points on a PowerPoint, which seems to have worked well, but does not lend itself to writing a book, since I could probably have summarised everything in five slides and done the subject a massive disservice. I do, however, enjoy telling and often repeating stories over a pint in the pub, and so it is the latter style I have attempted to draw on here.

Here's how this project started. A few months ago, I was listening to Richard Searling on Solar Radio doing a special show on Leeds Central, initially about the all-nighters and then the Central at large. Amongst others, he read out a letter I had sent in, along with that of my close friend Steve Caesar, and recounted some of the enjoyable nights he'd had personally at the Central and in particular the influence of the "legendary" Tony Banks. Richard also mentioned nobody had written much about the Central, to which in a moment of madness I thought, *I'll do that.*

Here's the email I sent to Richard:

Dear Richard,

Fantastic Friday nights with Twink, Swish, Paul Rowan and Frank (aka Ian Dewhirst) – always packed and sweaty, like a Soul club should be – dancing was tight, no room for backdrops and watch out for the low fan! Shout out to Jill, Cooky, Dangerous Dave, Oky, Caesar, Simon.

So many tunes, but special ones that spring to mind:

- Garnett Mimms – Looking For You
- Vibrations – Cause You're Mine
- Jades – Where It's At

Regards

Steve Taylor

In my usual ostentatious style, I told anyone who would listen of my intent to write a book on the subject, appreciating in a masochistic way that once I'd opened my big gob, I was committed.

I gave a lot of thought as to who I was writing this book for and came to the conclusion it's primarily for the people who attended the Central over the years and have fond memories of it. In addition, if it connects with other Northern Soul fans, highlighting similarities with their own clubs and experiences, that would be wonderful, and finally if it resonates with modern day clubbers, particularly those who frequent the HiFi, that would be an additional bonus.

There was much deliberation over the title with friends, with many great contenders, including *At the Discotheque*, *Something Keeps Calling Me Back* and *Going To A Happening*, but having completed the book, and reflecting on the many and varied references to the stairs, there could only be one winner: 'At The Top Of The Stairs' by the Formations. I suppose your view on its suitability depends on whether you mainly remember them going in or coming out, where "At the top of the stairs, there's darkness".

Another quandary was whether to include the interviews with DJs and dancers in their original format, using the dialogues and getting them into an order and form that those involved were happy to share, or alternatively to use these stories as material, eliminating the overlaps and slight discrepancies clouded by the mists of time, and cobbling it all together it one big story. I discounted the latter on the basis it would lose some of the authenticity, that the personal stories from many of the people who made the Central great deserved their own exposure, and that the end was worth a little repetition.

I conducted the interviews over many months, and true to my intent, it was like sitting down with old friends chatting over a few jars in a favourite pub, reminiscing about shared memories and experiences. Some of these people are actually close friends and hence it was reasonably easy, as I know them very well, and I've heard their stories so many times I can recite them almost as well they can, and in some cases much better. I won't name names because that would embarrass Simon Andrews. For others, particularly the original crowd I didn't know at the outset, I had some fabulous conversations, made all the more difficult because we couldn't see each other as we were in the midst of the Covid-19 pandemic. Despite that the conversations flowed, and they were only too happy to help and share their stories. I reciprocated with some of mine, and this made for an even livelier conversation, as we had encountered similar experiences, albeit at a slightly different time. Through this process, I got to know them and understand the massive role they played in forming and developing the club I came to love. For this I thank them, and now consider them friends. I look forward to a time we can all meet up in person at the Central, or perhaps beforehand at the Whitelocks, where I guess the beers are on me.

Here goes.

CHAPTER 1

AN INTRODUCTION TO THE CENTRAL

❀

If you are reading this, I'm guessing you've got some connection with Leeds Central, or you are really, really bored and reading a discarded copy somewhere. The Central played a big part in my formative years, and here is my attempt to capture some of the stories, music and spirit of those times.

But let's start at the very beginning...

The Central, or Central School of Dancing to give it its full title, started life in the 50s as a dance school and dance hall. It was located in the basement of 2 Central Road in Leeds, in my day across from the back of Woolworths and over the road from the Duncan pub. Its entrance was a narrow black and unmanned door, followed by an equally narrow and treacherous set of stairs, which led to yet another door that opened up into the hall. Once through the final door, you met with a manned booth type desk, where you paid your fee and entered into the dimly lit dancehall, with its wooden floors and supporting pillars. There was a small bar to the back left, a seating area to the back-right, and single rows of seating booths around the dance floor. I'm guessing in its day it was quite plush, but in the 70s it was a bit down at heel and in need of a facelift, not that we cared.

In the early 1940s, long before it was a dancehall, it was an amusement cellar called the Waxworks. Customers went down those same steps, and a lady in a booth charged a penny in exchange for a token, which could be used in the various machines. True to its name and arranged around the walls were wax images of various notorious murderers!

It was converted into the Central Dance Club in 1954 by Len Cave, a local entrepreneur and dance enthusiast, and dance classes were given initially by Jeanette and her husband, Walter. Classes took place on Wednesday afternoons as well as Saturday mornings and Sunday afternoons. Saturday evenings were for social dancing, and regulars report it being attended by "lovely people", but that the venue had a distinct odour, which wasn't stale beer but a "musky welcoming smell". People also refer to the treacherous steps even in those days. Joan Wood collected the cash on the desk by the door, with a "cheery smile and peroxide blond hair", and along with her husband, Derek, they also gave dance lessons. Joan and Derek stayed at the Central, managing it through the many changes in its function and clientele.

Len was a lean chap with a thin moustache, and only tended to come down at the weekends to play live on his Hammond style organ, which apparently, he had built himself and was his pride and joy. The organ was on a raised stage diagonally across from the entrance, with the bar to the left of it. The pillars were always an amusement to the dancers who had to dodge them, and the floor was wooden and nicely sprung. Bench-seated alcoves, complete with tables, were on the opposite wall to the entrance. Christmas and New Year were always very special and well attended, and there are numerous reports of the toilets being haunted, perhaps by the notorious waxwork murderers?

CHAPTER 2

THE EARLY SOUL YEARS

❀

The club began playing modern Beat music and attracting a younger dance crowd around '67. Len saw the changing market and the coffee bar scene, which was thriving around Leeds city centre, and wanted to attract some of that crowd, and importantly income, to the Central.

He dialled back the ballroom dancing (although it still continued through the week) and dedicated the weekend evenings to DJs and young dancers. Initially this was a mixed crowd of the youth cults of the day, predominantly mods and rockers, but this combination was never going to last.

There were several coffee bars around the town centre frequented by mods, often with their scooters lined up outside. One such café was La Concardora (the Conc) which later became Lulu's, a "bit of a dive" on Trinity walk, off Boar Lane. Its clientele were a mixture of mods, early skins and West Indians, all with an interest in the predominantly black music played in the cellar, but equally attracted by the edgy culture that persisted within. There was a core of 25 to 30 regulars, some with a reputation of being the hardest men in Leeds, and they formed a formidable gang, calling themselves the Lulu's. Some of their battles with rival gangs, particularly the one in Roundhay Park involving cricket bats, became immortalised in Leeds folk law and still persisted even when I became a regular in town some six years later.

The mod presence in the Central began to increase and pretty quickly precipitated into violence. Over several weeks, the mods, led by the Lulu's, battered the rockers into submission inside and outside the club until the rockers capitulated and retreated to the Star & Garter over the road. The mods now had the run of the Central.

From that point the music was exclusively for them, a mixture of Soul, Blue Beat, Ska and a smattering of the more R&B orientated white pop music, with a collection of DJs spinning the tunes. The Central owned and made available a sizable collection of records, all stamped "Leeds Central School of Dancing". Although there was a core of regular DJs, it was quite common for attendees to bring a box of records down and ask or be asked to do a spot.

The crowd continued to be multiracial, an exception in the day, partly facilitated by the doorman Willie (Bill) Richardson and his brother Tony, both of West Indian heritage. They were men of impressive size and stature, and Bill was something of a celebrity in Leeds and beyond, having had a long and successful career as a body builder, culminating in becoming Mr Universe in 1979. Other key figures were Joan and Derek Wood the managers, with Joan, a strong character, taking the lead role.

Other major Soul venues had closed; the Twisted Wheel in Manchester, the Bee-Gee and the old Mecca in Leeds, otherwise known as the Spinning Disc. These Soul boys and girls now had a lack of venues and started to make their way down to the Central. They had a thirst to hear the rare up-tempo Soul they had already experienced in other Soul clubs and started bringing some of their own records down to the club, badgering the DJs to play them.

The West Yorkshire DJs of the day, and Tony Banks in particular, saw and liked the general direction of travel in the music towards what they christened Uptown Soul, and pretty soon were digging into their own collections for records that fitted the bill (often B-sides) as well as acquiring the big tunes of the day from the record dealers, who were also congregating at the Central. The club quickly transitioned to become a 100% rare Uptown Soul venue, attracting crowds from far and wide, but unfortunately losing some of its original black crowd along the way, who preferring the funkier tunes which were now exploding onto the black music scene, and who migrated to another club at the bottom of Briggate called Primos.

All-nighters had been popular on the Northern Soul scene for some time, perhaps because this was the only time slot offered by the clubs who didn't want to displace the income from their existing clientele, or because the scene was underground and had national devotees travelling from Scotland, the Midlands and the South to attend the venues. Most Soul fans did not have access to cars, and hence getting to these often obscure locations was an ordeal in itself in those days, when your average person stayed within a few miles of their own house and didn't even venture into the local town centres, let alone travel hundreds of miles to different cities. Having got there, the Soul fans wanted and needed to stay for a good amount of time, and not face the hassle of attempting to get home in the middle of the night, preferring the convenience of jumping on trains and buses early next morning.

The Central organised a series of all-nighters at the beginning of '73, starting at 11pm on Saturday and finishing at 8 the next morning. Most of the regular Central crowd attended, although some of the younger ones could not establish convincing enough alibis to escape their parents. The Central had developed a bit of a reputation, and some parents didn't like their offspring attending, let alone hanging out all night there, which was certainly not the norm in the day. The DJs for the all-nighters were Keith Atkinson, Tony Banks "and friends".

At the second event, Richard Searling was added to the DJ roster. He had built his reputation at VaVa's in Bolton, and his addition attracted dancers from far and wide, augmenting the Central's expanding reputation as the place to be amongst the Soul crowd.

Amphetamines had become commonplace on the Northern scene in the form of slimming pills, which were widely available on prescription to those wishing to shed a few pounds, and were particularly prevalent at all-nighters, keeping attendees awake and fuelling their frenetic dancing. Green and Clears, Blueys, Chalkies, Duramin, Dexedrine and more all in circulation, often attained by the more wayward on the scene "screwing" chemists on their way to events to secure "gear" for themselves and others. This had not escaped the attention of the police, in fact had contributed to the closure of the Twisted Wheel in Manchester and the Golden Torch in Stoke-on-Trent. Many events had drug squad officers operating undercover, but they rarely got their dress or demeanour quite right, never dancing and looking very uncomfortable and out of place, easily identifiable, but still spreading paranoia across the club.

Towards the end of '73, at that fateful Leeds Central all-nighter, around 1am, 30 policemen stormed into the venue, ordered the lights to be switched on, the music to stop, and all the attendees to stay where they were and put their hands on their heads. People were forcefully frisked, and a general state of panic ensued. Pills scattered across the floor as pockets emptied before police had chance to search them. In total, 70 people were arrested that night and taken to Milgarth and other police stations around the city centre, many of them charged with possession of illegal drugs. A statement by Chief Superintendent Denis Hoban said: "Certain substances were seized and examined at Home Office forensic science laboratories. Those taken into custody were bailed and will appear in court at a later date. Many of those arrested were from outside Leeds area and a number had travelled from distant parts of the UK, including the South." Those naughty southerners.

That was the end of the all-nighters. The police had been unhappy with the licence to open all night in the first place, and had now successfully stopped them, despite their popularity, absence of violence (unlike the rest of Leeds city centre in those days) and the fact they were self-contained and not impacting the wider community. Granted, some of the customers were breaking the drug laws.

Fortunately, and despite police attempts, the club was allowed to continue to operate and importantly continue with Northern Soul nights, but within normal club licencing hours and subject to a membership scheme.

Tony Banks quite suddenly stopped as resident DJ, possibly due to a fall out with management, or perhaps he'd just had enough. He was quickly succeeded by Frank (Ian Dewhirst) and Twink (Ian Higginbottom), who had become Central regulars, Frank often lending some of his big records to Tony Banks to play. They were the resident DJs on the decks when I started attending in '74, aged 14 or 15.

CHAPTER 3

MY INITIATION ON TO THE NORTHERN SCENE

My introduction to Northern Soul like many others was through the youth club. In my case, this was Allerton Grange, where I went with a friend every Thursday evening. The usual mix of table tennis and table football, followed by a disco and the occasional romantic encounter or fracas (rarely with the same person at the same time). The music was the pop Soul and Reggae of the day, with particular favourites being Freda Payne's 'Band Of Gold', Chairman of the Board's 'Give Me Just A Little More Time', Lorna Bennet's 'Breakfast In Bed', Prince Buster's 'Al Capone', Susan Cadogan's 'Hurt So Bad', Pioneers 'Long Shot Kick De Bucket', and the unforgettably erotic Max Romeo's 'Wet Dream'.

At a certain point in the night, the music changed to a more upbeat and obscure kind of Soul, the dancefloor cleared, and a couple of lads started fast shoe shuffling and spinning on the floor. They wore wide-legged high-waisted bags, bowling shirts and highly polished smooth brogue type shoes. Their feet seemed to float across the floor, they reached for the sky and clapped at set points in the music and were confidently oblivious to the awestruck onlookers. In my memory were tunes like Chuck Wood's '7 Days Too Long', Casualeers' 'Dance, Dance, Dance' and Tony Clarke's 'Landslide'. The music was fast and pumping and unknown to me at the time. I didn't know what this phenomenon was, I just knew it was cool and exciting and I wanted to be part of it.

On one such night, I was standing close to the entrance of the club when in walked three lads I didn't know, older than me and clearly intoxicated. As older readers will recall, you could not officially get into regular clubs until age 21, so lots of 16 – 18-year-olds went to the pub and then to the youth clubs. I must have glanced at one of them, to which came the popular question of the day, "What are you looking at?" to be met be the equally popular, but under the circumstances rather dangerous reply, "Not a lot". Next thing I know, I'm fighting with them in the middle of the floor and getting battered, when in jumped a lad I had never met before to help me out. It turns out this was Dave Raby, who didn't like this lot, enjoyed a scrap, and was rather good at it. Dave later became a very good amateur boxer and "could have been somebody, he could have been a contender". He also had a keen interest in Northern Soul and remains a close friend to this day. When I saw a similar scene in Elaine Constantine's *Northern Soul* film, I could have choked on my popcorn! Surely that scene was based on me and Dave and had been passed down the annals of Northern Soul history? It couldn't have been a coincidence or such a common occurrence, could it?

I could write another book on the exploits of Dave and I on the Northern scene over the years, but I'll save that for my sequel. Just to give you a flavour, we were in the Wilton Ballroom near Castleford about 10 years ago, when someone we didn't know came up to Dave and asked, "Did you chin them lads on Manchester station who were kicking soulies' holdalls on the way to Wigan in about 1976?" Dave modestly replied, "Aye, that wo me." Sure enough, we had been on that station waiting for the Wigan train. All of the Soul fans were lined up on the platform with the holdalls on the ground. A couple of local yobs walked along the line, kicking the bags and generally abusing the soulies, when they came to Dave and I at the end. The main culprit squared up to Dave, and the next minute was making Bruce Lee noises and adopting Kung Fu stances. I must admit, I thought we were in a spot of bother, but then the "Fists of Fury" flew (Dave's) and the wannabe martial artist was out cold. His mate made a half-hearted attempt to intervene, so I helped him on his way with a well-placed and deserved kick up the arse. The joys of running the gauntlet to get to Wigan Casino in the early 70s, but it was all worth it once we got there.

Dave and I started hanging out at Jumbo Records on Saturday afternoon, owned by Hunter and Lornette, which specialised in Black music, had some of the latest Northern Soul releases, and was always full of interesting and knowledgeable characters. We also went to Virgin Records on Kirkgate. The Hairies all went upstairs for their Led Zeppelin and Pink Floyd, but downstairs was all Soul, and Carl the guy behind the counter was very helpful and knowledgeable. Pinned on the wall each week were original copies of 50 or so records, all in stock for 25p, from Jackie Lee 'Oh My Darling' to Diane Jenkins 'Towaway Zone', each with a little handwritten label by Carl telling us a bit about the disc and where it had first been played. I still have a hundred or so records from Virgin, which now go for a bit more than 25p. I remember Carl pulling out a big pile of red and yellow British Action label 45s one Saturday, but foolishly I only bought one; John Roberts 'I'll Forget You', for 50p. If I could turn back the hands of time.

I'm guessing we heard about the Central in Virgin or Jumbo, and Dave and I arranged to go one Friday night. We first met in the Precinct pub on Kirkgate, somewhere else we'd heard was frequented by Soul boys. At the back of the pub was a dance floor shaped a bit like an MMA ring, and sometimes acting as one, where the crowd danced to Funk and Reggae. The Northern Soul crowd tended to congregate in the front bar, but both crowds mixed amicably, and this is where my eclectic taste for all things soulful was probably developed. We had a couple of pints (well, we were only 15) before moving down to the Central early doors.

At the bottom of the stairs, we were sombrely met by Derek Wood, who asked to see our memberships. We probably tried to blag it and say we'd forgotten them but were simply asked to complete new cards. That's it, we were in. The place was fairly quiet, with most punters still in the pub, but we wanted to suss it out and settle in. There were some fabulous old tunes being played, such as Bobby Bland 'Call On Me' (I still have a copy stamped "Central School of Dancing" that I somehow acquired along the way), Jackie Wilson's 'Nothing But Blue Skies' and Major Lance 'The Beat'. It turned out this DJ was Twink, and as my knowledge and appreciation for the music grew, I began to recognise his excellent taste. Even as the years went by, we regularly turned up early to hear his first set.

As we got to know the club and its layout, it became clear there were different zones. A lot of the older crowd sat down in the area with tables and chairs directly opposite the entrance, and rarely danced. Although we got to know and get along with most of them (for example Spud, a very nice fella and fireman, sadly no longer with us) some I'm guessing by their demeanour didn't like us young upstarts being there, seemingly more interested in the seedier drug side of the equation than the music and made us feel a little unwelcome. Luckily, they were a very small minority, besides which we didn't give a shit. The irreverence of youth.

There was in those days an edgier side to the Northern scene and some of its followers, and one or two even dabbled with far-right politics in the late 70s, which brought us into direct confrontation. I have always found it an oxymoron that we have a small number of racist Northern Soul fans in our midst. How can you be a Soul fan of any genre without empathising with the struggle of the people who made the music and admiring their rich culture that stemmed from it? You still hear occasional voices in the Northern Soul forums and from a particular weekender promotor, and even on a Soul radio station uttering thinly veiled racism, particularly following the murder of George Floyd and the Black Lives Matter protests that manifested from it. The Soul radio incident was swiftly dealt with by the station owner, much to his credit, and the culprit sacked. Only when black lives matter equally, in all aspects of society, can anyone say with any integrity that all lives matter. These few should be ostracised from the scene, or at least educated.

The flip side of this are those of us, the vast majority, who despite being white wore black Soul power fists on our badges, around

11

our necks, and tattooed on our skin, and the genuine heartfelt passion, empathy and support we feel for social and racial justice. We could perhaps relate in some small way with the inequalities and injustices faced by black America with the challenges we faced in our own lives, the majority of people on the scene originating from working class backgrounds. The music provided a cathartic release, telling us impassioned stories of love and heartbreak. This up-tempo Soul music, that brought its messages of hope and positivity to young black America, did the same for us. We were truly Soul brothers and sisters.

The better dancers seemed to congregate around the DJ area, while the crowd I associated with were towards the back left corner. The people I remember were obviously my mates Dave Raby and Steve Cook, along with big Mally, "Jack" Horner, little Melv, Gary (aka Sam), Denise, Lynne & Diane, Michell, Jeff, Shef, Robert, Sally Ann, Janet, Jill, Jack, Blake and Craig. Embarrassingly, when the reunions started, I didn't recognise Craig Robinson due to senility, several pints and being blinded by bright sunshine while consuming the beer outside the Adelphi before descending into the dungeon-like darkness of the Central. I am delighted to say that once I got home and thought about it, I did remember Craig, who had hardly changed over the years, unlike me, who had turned grey and lost most of my hair. Luckily, he became a Facebook friend and sent me pictures of what he used to look like back in the day, and I apologised the next time I saw him. He has forgiven me, and we keep in contact.

Another notable character was Cockney Steve, a passionate Leeds United fan, as most of us were, but perhaps not quite as passionate as Steve. He stood 6'3" with a big afro and long black leather coat, and as his nickname suggests, hailed from London. In later years I asked Steve what had brought him to Leeds in the first place, and he said, "To fight for Leeds United." To that end, he was successful. Steve Luigi tells a funny story about Steve. They were allegedly jumping the train to a venue in Scarborough, or somewhere like that, and jumped the barrier at the other end. The guards ran after them and eventually caught them, and said they'd seen Steve jumping the barrier, to which he replied, "How do you know it was me?" Clearly a case of mistaken identity.

Steve Luigi became an early acquaintance and occasionally we joined him on trips to Wigan. He had an old banger, and on one fateful trip it broke down somewhere before we crossed the Pennines. Dave and I got out to push while Steve steered us down the slip road. The car picked up speed, and Dave and I jumped on the back as Steve tried to bump it off. The engine picked up, and Steve sped around the roundabout at the bottom, apparently unaware that Dave and I were still clinging on for dear life! Come on, Steve, all is forgiven, but you did know we were on the back, didn't you? On the way home from Wigan the next day, the bloody thing broke down again. We were stranded at the side of the M62 when a car of Asian lads stopped and asked if we needed help. There were already six in the car, but they happily agreed to take us three with them back to Bradford. It was a bit tight to say the least, but thanks to their kindness, they got three very tired and miserable lads home.

Some of the music in those early days was a bit old style R&B for my taste, the likes of Bill Blacks Combo – Little Queenie and Ace Cannon – Sea Cruise, and to my ignorant ears sounded like Rock 'n' Roll, music we associated with old Teddy Boys who were still knocking around the city centre, the antithesis of the modernistic Soul scene we were beginning to love. I was much more interested in the soulful vocal tracks, some of which I list below, along with trying not to embarrass myself on the dancefloor as I crept onto it, becoming less conspicuous and self-conscious as the floor filled. I had practised and practised my dancing on the kitchen lino in my socks at home, playing taped records that I'd acquired or borrowed and trying to emulate the lads I'd seen at the youth club, twisting one foot from side to side and letting the other drag along, trying to change the step a little, so I didn't look like some demented caged animal you'd often see at the zoo, pacing one way and then the other.

I'm not the world's greatest dancer, but my dance has stood me in good stead over the years, taking me through the stompers, slowing a little for the mecca tunes, and then shortening the lateral movement and more stepping on the spot for the soulful disco stuff. In fact, I do similar dance to Modern Soul and Soulful House, and have occasionally been complimented by those who don't know any better on what a lovely mover I am. Unfortunately, all that twisting has played havoc with the knees and hips, and although I still love to dance, I do need more of a sit down between tunes these days. I'm sure "Northern Soul Knee" could be classified as an official medical condition, and I'm equally sure I'm not the only sufferer.

On the subject of dancing, the origins of Northern Soul dancing have often been commented on. In my view one does not need to look any further than early footage of Jackie Wilson and James Brown, with their fast one-footed shuffles and tight spins. I'm guessing this was copied by the early mods and brought into the north's Soul clubs such as the Twisted Wheel in Manchester, and it developed from there, as dancers coolly battled for supremacy out on the floor, adding their own bespoke moves but never stooping to acknowledge they were competing with each other.

This was undoubtedly the origins of the Central style of Northern Soul dancing, where the footwork and movement had to be tight due to the lack of space. There were no high kicks or backdrops at the Central, as jumps would run the risk of hitting the ceiling, or worse still, getting decapitated by the low-hanging ceiling fans. If you attempted a backdrop or floor work, you were likely to get trampled underfoot, never to be seen again. The finest exponents of this Central style were Eric Smith and Steve Caesar. I can still picture Eric in his long leather coat (who must have been sweating cobs) floating across the floor, and Steve Caesar (who incidentally became the 1974 Wigan Casino dance champion) gyrating and spinning in his organic and flowing style. Other notable dancers were Ian Muscroft and David Okonofau, who introduced a Blackpool Mecca funkier style and leg movements that defy gravity. Steve Luigi I've got to say was also good, with his fast on

14

the spot footwork and high-speed spins; it's no wonder his knees are knackered! I'm sure we've all got our favourite dancers, but one thing's for sure is that Central soulies have their own unique style that can be spotted anywhere even after all these years.

I suppose in the early days we were all captivated by the youth cult of Northern Soul (I certainly was) but over the years we have become less impressed with this aspect, as it was hard to be cool even in your 30s, let alone 60s, and the music and culture surrounding it have become part of who we are. I was 15 and impressionable, and the early scene was magical to me. It felt prideful, and I suppose a little elitist, to be accepted and be part of this underground and exclusive club. The older lads looked sharp in their tailormade suits, brogues and oxford shirts and short side-parted hair, later grown out into a longer centre-parted styles. The dancing was impressive and super cool, and they couldn't care less that "divs" (non-soulies) might have thought them effeminate to be dancing at all, when at other venues most males stood around dancefloors, pint in hand like wallflowers, watching the girls dance around their handbags. They would never be called effeminate to their faces, however, because many of these lads could handle themselves and were some of the hardest around, which all added to the mystique and attraction of the scene.

My early attire was acquired as a young suedehead at Class, a shop at the bottom of Briggate. They stocked all the two-tone and Prince of Wales checked trousers and Ben Sherman button-down collars, then later high-waister oxford bags and bowling shirts, which had become the rigour of the day for Soul fans. I later found some fabulous old men's shirts in a shop off one of the arcades (I can't remember what it was called, but I think it's where I also got a copy of Bob & Earl's *Harlem Shuffle* album for 50p) which had a straight bottom and pyjama collar, just right for the scene and only costing a couple of pounds.

As we became bolder and more in tune with the Soul fashions, Dave and I would get cloth from Leeds market and take it to

Trew's the tailors on the Headrow, designing our own suits. They were typically high-fastening, three buttons, narrow lapel, double vented at the back with side flap pockets and a ticket pocket on the right-hand side. Trousers were double front pleated, about 12" wide and parallel, two flap pockets at the back, two slant pockets at the side, ticket pocket and waist adjuster grips, cut just to the top of our shoes, which were smooth brown brogue style or a kind of pleated top black brogue (which I think we got from a shop in Wakefield) all with leather soles for slipping around, Art Freeman style.

CHAPTER 4

TIME MARCHES ON

There were always incidents that occurred around the Central visits. One night Dave and I were making our way home to where we had arranged to get a taxi, down by Leeds outdoor market stalls. Out of nowhere jumped two morons, intent on battering us as part of their evening's entertainment. The lead moron picked up a brick, and in response, Dave somehow magicked up a big stick. Seeing we were not going to run, lead moron started to lose his bravado and philosophically said, "Look, you've got a stick, I've got a brick, why don't we leave it?" to which Dave and I broke into a spontaneous rendition of the Dean Parrish classic, "Nothing but bricks, broken bottles and sticks everywhere." The morons bottled it and left muttering, "You're fucking mad, you two." They had a point.

On another such night, Cooky and I had left our scooters on the street behind Milgarth police station. It was a nice quiet street, and our thinking was they'd be safe with the constabulary looking on. No such luck. On returning after the Central, someone had smashed up Cooky's scooter but luckily left mine, presumably because they were spotted. They had literally folded his side panels in half! We were furious, and Jill went into a big rant about how low these people were, what morons and what possessed them to carry out such a despicable act, finishing with, "We should go and find some motorbikes and smash them up!" If you know Jill, you'll recognise how out of character that was, the irony lost on her, however it diffused the situation a little for Cooky and I, and we fell about laughing.

We had parked the scooters there another night, and as usual hid the helmets and parkas in the privet hedge at the side of the street, to save us having to take them to the Central. On returning after the night out, we searched the hedge for our gear, but to no avail. As we looked around in puzzlement, wondering if it had been another hedge, a policeman leaned out of the 3rd floor at Milgarth and shouted, "Looking for these, lads?" I've got to say we were a little tipsy (don't frown, drink driving was less socially unacceptable in those days) and having to walk into the station to get our stuff back was not an easy thing to do. Luckily there was no issue, and the policeman gave them back and said we should put them in the cloakroom next time. Phew!

Leaving behind the folly of my youth, the things that have endured the test of time have been the music and lifelong friendships formed on the scene. It's hard to describe the feeling I got and still get when I hear the music, the searing and impassioned vocals sending tingles of emotion down my spine and the driving beat moving my feet to dance, telling tales of love affairs, heartache, and the hardship of life in the ghettos of black America, but I'm guessing you feel the same. These records are ingrained in my brain. There are tunes I've not heard for over 40 years that I still know word for word and like to sing along to while dancing, much to the annoyance of everyone around me, or at least my version of the words. Am I the only one who made up their own words? For example, I always thought the Pointer Sisters 'Send Him Back' went along the lines of "send him back, send my baby back, send him along right back, send my baby back," when apparently it is "send him back, send my baby back, shooby be do do do, send my baby back". Personally, I prefer my version.

I have tried to think about specific tunes at specific periods but struggled a little due to the elapse of time. However, here is my list of Central tunes from my early years in no particular order of preference (except for perhaps the first two, favourites of mine):

- Jackie Lee – Oh My Darling
- Moses Smith – Girl Across The Street
- J J Barnes – Sweet Sherry

- Garnet Mimms – Looking For You
- Edwin Starr – Backstreets
- Hesitations – I'm Not Built That Way
- Showstoppers – What Can A Man Do
- Vibrating Vibrations – Surprise Party
- Little Richard – I Don't Wanna Discuss It
- Vibrations – Gonna Get Along Without You Now
- J J Barnes – Real Humdinger
- Major Lance – Investigate
- Al De Lory – Right On
- Donald Height – Talk Of The Grapevine
- Spellbinders – Help Me
- Tony Clarke – Landslide
- J J Barnes – Please Let Me In
- Tommy Neal – Going To A Happening
- James Barnett – Keep On Talking
- Edwin Starr – I Have Faith In You
- Chuck Jackson – Chains Of Love
- Incredibles – There's Nothing Else To Say
- Impressions – You've Been Cheating
- Lou Johnson – Unsatisfied
- Shirley Ellis – Soul Time
- James Carr – That's All I Want To Know
- Jerry Williams – If You Ask Me
- Cliff Nobles – Our Love Is Getting Stronger
- Barbara Mills – Queen Of Fools
- Billy Butler – Right Track
- Bunny Sigler – Don't Make Me Wait
- Olympics – Same Old Thing
- Jackie Wilson – Nothing But Blue Skies
- Johnny Moore – Walk Like A Man
- Willie Kendrick – Change Your Ways
- Art Freeman – Slipping Around
- Al Wilson – Help Me
- Lee David – Temptation Is Calling My Name
- Johnny Jones – Purple Haze
- Artistics – Hope We Have

- Williams and Watson – Too late
- Laura Lee – To Win Your Heart
- Philip Mitchel – Free For All
- Roy Hamilton – Cracking Up
- Dean Courtney – I'll Always Love You
- Dobie Gray – Out On The Floor
- Otis Smith – Let Her Go
- Jackie Wilson – The Whispers Getting Louder
- Al Kent – The Way You've Been Acting Lately
- Major Lance – You Don't Want Me No More
- Christine Cooper – Heartaches Away My Boy
- Homer Banks – Open The Door To Your Heart
- Jerry Butler – Moody Woman
- Formations – At The Top Of The Stairs
- Elgins – Heaven Must Have Sent You
- Millie Jackson – My Man Is A Sweet Man
- Frankie Beverely – If That's What You Wanted
- Isley Brothers – Tell Me It's Just A Rumour
- Jimmy Soul Clark – Sweet Darlin
- Darryl Stewart – Name It And Claim It
- Soul Twins – Quick Change Artist
- Saxi Russel – Psychedelic Soul
- Bob Relf – Blowing My Mind To Pieces
- Stanley Mitchel – Get It Baby
- Sam & Kitty – I've Got Something Good
- Duke Browner – Crying Ove You
- Eddie & Ernie – I Just Can't Do It
- Four Perfections – I'm Not Strong Enough
- Thelma Lyndsey – Prepared To Love You
- Saphires – Slow Fizz
- Jackie Lee – Darkest Days
- First Choice – This Is The House
- Jo Amstead – I Feel A Hurt Coming On

I could go on and on, but these are the tunes that spring to my mind in those early formative years. Incredible music and incredible times that will stay with me forever. These classics were played by DJs Frank, Twink and Swish, who had built their collections and taste from the Torch years. Sadly, I never got to hear Tony Banks play, but his memories will be captured later as others recount their stories.

It wasn't all dance, dance, dance at the Central, we also had a healthy interest in members of the opposite sex, and over the weeks as familiarity grew and better options exhausted, we'd get to talk to them and occasionally enter into romantic encounters. I will not name names, to protect the not so innocent, but the most attractive of them all to me, honest, was Jill Day (as was) my long-suffering wife.

She would go down with her mates, Jane and Joanne, and shuffle around in the opposite corner to us. I liked the look of her and loved the way she dressed a bit different, in funkier and more avant-garde clothes, and also the way she acted a little aloof, which she now tells me was shyness. The first time I tried to talk to her at the Central she blanked me, with what I perceived as her nose in the air.

As luck would have it a few weeks later, Dave and I were on the train travelling back from the all-nighter at Wigan. We saw the guard coming up the carriage, and since we didn't have tickets to hand, we made our way to the toilet. As we did so, who should we see running the other way, but the girls we'd admired from the Central, Jill and Jane, who had also misplaced their tickets. The four of us all crammed quickly into the toilet, and when the guard hammered on the door demanding to see tickets, Dave politely explained that he was having a bowel movement if the chap wouldn't mind kindly leaving him to it, or words to that effect. When we got off the train in Leeds, the ice was broken, and we all got to know each other a little. Unfortunately for me, Dave walked Jill to her bus, and I went the other way with Jane (no offence, Jane), but the following week at the Central, Jill and I got talking, and following a snog in the taxi queue at city station, forty-odd years, two children and two grandchildren, she still talks to me occasionally, although probably won't after disclosing this story.

As time moved on, Frank became the main DJ, bringing a more modern style of Northern, a funkier Mecca sound, along with some rare stompers he discovered. Frank was tall with curly black hair and a bit older than us. Even in those days, he was a more professional DJ with an almost American microphone style which you could actually hear, despite originating from Mirfield, whereas all you could generally hear from most of the others was a muffled rant, and if you were lucky a few syllables from the title which you'd try and decipher later. Ian says jokingly it was due to having southern parentage.

CHAPTER 5

THE DJs

❁

Denis Billingham's story:

I was into Soul music from around 1965; from the age of 15 I'd already caught the bug. I started DJing at Leeds Central in 1968 and carried through until the opening of Hernies Club in 1971. This was for me the beginning of a Soulful adventure, taking me far and wide, collecting music, finding some of the undiscovered tunes that are known and loved today, and creating the opportunity to meet and work with lots of the artists I idolised. The Central was my hometown starting point for my journey.

When I first went to the Central, the people who went there were a bit of a mixed crowd. The club was more associated with being a ballroom dance school that doubled up as a Rock and Roll and Beat music club, as opposed to a Soul music venue. Willie was the very large doorman, and one of his favourite records was 'These Drums' by Willie Nelson, so that gives you a flavour of some of the things played back then. The places in Leeds to hear mod and Soul music at that time were the Bee-Gee, the Iowanas Club or the old Mecca, all purveyors of great danceable Soul music, which was known in those early days as Uptown Soul. I was going to the Twisted Wheel and Catacombs Top Twenty at the time, so my grounding in Soul was pretty solid.

When I first started at the Central there were three resident DJs; Andy Harrison, myself, and another guy whose name, for the life of me, I can't remember. Andy would play Motown, Stax, Atlantic, our mystery friend would play more pop and rock 'n' roll type things, and I would play similar to Andy, but with more emphasis on Uptown Soul. The whole ethos of the club changed over the months and years that followed as more and more Soul music was played. The people from the Bee-Gee and old Mecca all started to come down and join the fun, along with the Soul crowds from other local areas: Barnsley, York, Halifax, Selby and further afield.

My enjoyable time at the Central ended in 1971, by which time it had become well established as a good Northern Soul club, playing high-quality Soul music, such as the Invitations – 'What's Wrong With Me Baby', American Poets, Chuck Jackson – 'Chains Of Love', Otis Redding – 'Look At That Girl', Little Richard – 'I Don't Wanna Discuss It', Incredibles – 'Nothing Else To Say', Joy Lovejoy – 'In Orbit', Bobby Bland – 'Call On Me', Ad Libs – 'Nothing Worse Than Being Alone', O'Jays – 'I Dig Your Act', Errol Dixon – 'I Walk', Lou Rawls, Eagle, Dean Parrish – 'Nothing But Bricks', Ronnie Milsap, Jimmy Radcliffe, Leon Haywood – 'Baby Reconsider', the list was endless and all pretty cutting edge in the day.

I was also DJing at a few other places at this time, the Metro in Wakefield, L'Ambassadeur in Bradford, and a stint at Blazes in Stockport. My parting of the ways with the Central and Joan, came about when myself and Mick Eastwood opened a Soul club in Harehills Leeds called Hernies. Joan saw this as direct competition and did not want me to DJ at both places, so I left to start up Hernies. This proved to be a great success, even though it was pretty short lived, as the Leeds Drug Squad decided to raid and close the club one Saturday all-nighter. Joan did offer me my residency at the Central back several times after Hernies closed, but I never did go back, preferring to continue my journey further afield.

Over the years since that time, I have, in the pursuit of our beloved Northern Soul music, travelled extensively and met many people, working in the music studios of Chicago, having a DJ residency at a club in the centre of the recording studios in Chicago, where many of the artists who were working locally would call in and chat. I was in dreamland. I stayed with Bobby Bland for the best part of three months; what more could you wish for?

I have also promoted several successful venues over the years, in constant pursuit of providing great music, including the Concorde Suite in Droylsden and the Bridge Hall Hotel in Bury. At one point, Brian Rae and myself even tried to revive the Whitworth Street Twisted Wheel, back in the '90s, and although we managed to have a few successful nights, all-dayers and one all-nighter, we were unable to secure enough regular dates to move it forward. Further down the line, Pete Roberts obviously had more luck with the owners, and managed to revive Whitworth Street back to the powerhouse it once was. Of all the venues I have DJ'd at over the years, my all-time favourite was the Twisted Wheel. During this period of time, I was involved with West Coast Promotions, along with Mark Bicknell and Pete Hollander, and the three of us can proudly lay claim to being the first people to bring both Barbara Acklin and Ruby Andrews over from the States to perform for the first time in the UK.

The record collecting and pursuit of rare Soul music continues and probably always will. My philosophy for DJing has never changed throughout; play quality danceable Soul music, play something popular, play something rare, play something unissued, play something unknown, and most importantly, play OVO! I always felt a bit of a responsibility to entertain, but also to try and educate, to take people on a musical journey. If I played a set where everyone knew everything, I felt I hadn't done my job; I had no barriers, as long as it was soulful and danceable.

The Central was the starting place, and I feel proud to have been the first DJ to have played proper Northern Soul down there, my first real venture into DJing, and so it will always hold a soft spot for me. In the early days of the Central, there was great music played, and it was influential across the north, I don't think it got the recognition it deserved.

Long live the Leeds Central, and I hope to see everyone on a dance floor sometime in the near future.

Keith Atkinson's story:

I left school in the summer of 1967 and got a job in the city of Leeds as an apprentice jeweller. There was a guy worked there called Barry Kajzik, who sort of took me under his wing and showed me the job. We got on really well, and one Friday he asked if I wanted to come out for a drink, saying he knew a place where there'd be lots of girls and we could have a few pints.

So off I went down to the Central School of Dancing. Joan ran it and taught ballroom dancing through the day, and at night opened it as a nightclub disco. Back then the law said you had to join and have a membership card, much like working men's club. We started to go down on a regular basis, and I soon made friends with other likeminded guys, such as Chris Mallows, Tony Jackson and Dave Maltas.

We found that we all had a love for Soul music – Stax, Tamla Motown – and we would always be bugging the DJs to play these sorts of records. The guys who were the DJs played a mixture of chart records and some Soul, but we'd also take our records down and ask them to play them. I can't remember their real names, but we used to call one of them Chicken Fat Charlie, because he always drank a load of beer, and then after the club, go for chicken and chips. He was a friend of Barry's and knew Joan.

I remember things like The Hollies and that awful Rod Stewart record being played. Fortunately, one night one of the DJs went to Joan and said he was leaving, and then Barry came up to me and said Joan would like a word. There was a really small scullery at the back of the club near the toilets, where Joan and her daughter sat, and that's where the discussion took place.

She said, "Barry tells me you have a lot of records; would you like to DJ?" I was quite shy back then, so initially I said no. Barry then had a word with me, and I changed my mind, saying I'd give it a go. The following week I was down with a box of records, DJ'd for a couple of weeks, and then the other guy said he was also packing it in, so Joan asked me if I knew anyone else who could DJ. I said yes and introduced Tony Jackson to Joan. We asked her if we could turn it into a Soul club and play more of the records we all liked, and to her credit she said yes, but if we didn't get the numbers we'd have to go back to how it was before, that she had a business to run. That is how the Central Soul Club was born.

A lot of the regular customers were disgruntled at first and kept asking us to play this and that, but we stuck to the Soul. There was a bit of a battle of wills and fists for a few weeks, but we got our way. Willie Richardson was the bouncer, and he'd stand on the door eating fruit. He'd stick his hand out to shake yours and took great delight in teasing you and crushing your fingers. He was a big strong fella.

Me and Tony Jackson DJ'd for a year or two, but the demand for the rarer records grew and grew and we didn't have the money for them. That's when Tony Banks came on the scene. He just turned up out of the blue. Joan told us she still wanted us to DJ, but that she'd got another DJ, Tony Banks, and that he was going to do a spot. He was a professional DJ and had some top sounds that we didn't have, and to be fair he had an incredible collection of British demos and imports. Tony Banks was a character, very quiet and kept himself to himself. They say I'm quiet, but I tried to talk to him and would get one-word answers. As soon as he'd finish his spot, he'd lock up his records and go, he didn't really socialise.

I got most of my records from Jumbo. I'd be in there every Friday lunchtime and spend most of my weekly wage. I got a discount from Hunter as I was DJing. I liked to collect labels, Invictus for example, some of which I've never played. I also bought Soul packs from Soul Bowl and got a copy of Wade Fleming's 'Jeanette' in one. I can't remember if I played it at the time, but certainly didn't appreciate its rarity. Some of my favourite tunes were

Alice Clarke, Poppies, Rex Garvin – 'Grooving At The Go Go', Parliaments – 'Don't Be Sore At Me', Duke Browner – 'Crying Over You', Edwin Star – 'Time'.

I was at the all-nighter the night of the raid, and we were commanded to put our hands on our heads as the police came charging down the stairs. We all got carted off to a police station and had to give a urine sample. When I got released, I didn't know where the hell I was, but two other lads came out and said they knew, so off we went and walked back into town, back to the Central to pick up the stuff we had left behind. I got a letter a few months later saying I would not be prosecuted.

Tony Banks left as suddenly as he had arrived. I heard he'd asked for more money and Joan told him where to go. You didn't mess with Joan. That's when Ian and Twink got involved.

The Central meant everything to me at the time; if I'd have been a millionaire, I would have bought it, I just loved the place. It wasn't like other clubs, where they'd be fighting in lumps. You never got that at the Central, you'd get hugs and kisses, and it's still like that today.

I stopped going in the summer of '76 because that's when I met my wife, and she wasn't into it.

Tony Jackson's story:

I heard about the Central from my brother Kevin, who was four years older than me, a big Soul fan, and he'd go down there when it was a mod club, when Willie was on the door. I went down when I was 15 and Andy Harrison was DJing, I think on Fridays and Sundays, and I soon became a regular. I was familiar with some of the tunes from hearing stuff my brother played at home, and the hairs on the back of my neck would stand up, the atmosphere was electric. I'd constantly go up to Andy to ask what the tunes were, I was like a sponge soaking up as much as I could. I started to build a small collection, and had access to my brother's records, and eventually Andy asked if I'd do a spot for an hour. This would have been around '69 – '70. I've still got records with "Central School of Dancing" stamped on them, as do several others, which must have been owned by the venue at some point but have somehow ended up in our collections. I've got a Doris Troy – 'I'll Do Anything' with the stamp on it. There's a lad called Dave who has gone one better: he's got a piece of the original Central dancefloor!

I don't know what happened to Andy, whether he'd got into trouble or something, but he disappeared for a while. He was always smartly dressed in suits; his uncle owned a tailors. At that time Joan the manageress approached me, Keith Atkinson and Chris Mallows and asked if we wanted to play. We didn't call it Northern Soul in the day, I think we called it Uptown Soul. Most of the stuff we played in the early days was Motown, Stax, Atlantic, American imports. We'd started going to the Torch and various Yorkshire venues, so we were hearing stuff there, trying to find out what it was and bringing it back to the Central. No one had cars, so we typically travelled by train.

The decks were not like those of today, where the speed is instant, in those days they started slowly, which took a particular skill, and there was no listening and cueing in, you just had to guess. We were young kids, and this was all new and exciting, we were just learning. Favourite tunes for me at the time were Chris Jackson – 'I'll Never forget you', Barbara Mills – 'Queen Of Fools', Saxie Russell – 'Psychedelic Soul', Rufus Lumley – 'I'm Standing', Darrell Banks – 'Angel Baby', Art Freeman – 'Slipping Around', Formations – 'At The Top Of The Stairs'. Looking back, we were playing many of what is now referred to as the "Top 500", all the things that have become classics, these were the big tunes at the time, they were being played at all the top venues.

Jumbo Records opened on the balcony in the Queens Arcade, and we got most of the new releases there. Hunter Smith would play us stuff, and if we liked it, we'd buy it.

Because the Central was in the city centre and easy to get to, we started getting people from further afield. They'd be going to different venues and start asking for tunes they'd heard there, many of which we didn't have at the time, but we did our best to acquire them. We were all young apprentices in our day jobs, so didn't have a lot of money to buy everything. There was obviously no eBay or internet, so sourcing the records was tough. That's really why we started bringing in guest DJs, to help out. Tony Banks was the first big one.

Tony Banks was really into American stuff, not just music but also American cars. He wore a baseball cap, with this long frizzy ginger hair sticking out. He was a professional DJ, and his collection was incredible, he was much older than us. After Tony left, that's when Frank and Twink became the main DJs, which coincided with most of us moving on to other aspects of our lives.

Many years later, in the early 80s, I saw an advert in the Yorkshire Post for a Northern night at the Cherry Tree pub in Leeds with Tony Banks. I wondered if it was the same fella, so went down to check it out. It was him, but there was hardly anyone there, so I went up and had a chat. He took my phone number on the premise that if he was doing another gig, he'd give me a call. I'd get a phone call every week, and you'd be on the phone for an hour or more, and he'd talk and talk and then right at the end, he'd tell you about a venue he was doing, which I'm guessing was the reason for the call in the first place. He started Brighouse before Ginger.

Our crowd back in the day was Roy Adams, Chris Mallows, Dave Maltas, Steve Luigi and Pete Dillon. We used to go to other venues together and someone got a coach trip together to go to the Torch. Great days and I don't envy the kids these days – to some extent it's all on a plate, they don't have to travel, but then they don't get to meet people from other places, and the lockdown is terrible for them.

After losing a friend to prostate cancer, myself and a few friends decided to put on some Northern Soul gigs to raise money to help find a cure. We are now a registered charity called CHARITY SOUL, which is entirely run by volunteers. So far, we've raised and donated over £104k, holding events around the country, as well as two weekenders in Spain. For more info about us, please go to our website https://charity-soul.co.uk/

I enjoy the reunions, but the crowd is changing again. Some of the old crowd have stopped coming, there's a lot of new faces, but everyone seems to be enjoying themselves, although the music hasn't really moved on much. There's plenty of stuff still out there. Back in the day, we'd have turned our nose up at them because they were too slow, but now they're perfect for our ageing bodies to shuffle along to. The 100mph stuff might kill someone these days, give them a heart attack!

The Central was my life at that time, my first love. It's where I learnt about Soul music, where I grew up, and I thank my lucky stars I was part of it. There's nowhere that's ever really had the same atmosphere, it was very compact, and you got to know everyone.

Twink's story:

I originally come from Cleckheaton, which is not far away, and one of our gang mentioned they were going to the Central and did I want to come along. I'd heard of it before and I knew people that had been, but I'd been a bit of a country bumpkin, and although Leeds was nearby, it seemed like a major journey in those days. This would have been about '71. I saw the tail end of Tony Banks DJing.

I was DJing all over the place before I went to the Central, and when I got down there, I started talking to a few people and they asked if I wanted to spin a few. Of course, I said yes, and next thing you know I'm DJing every week. This was '72, I think.

31

Ian came slightly after me, he's a couple of years younger, I'm 70 next year. I'm putting two and two together, but I think when Tony Banks left, there was a bit of a hole, and that's when the management said they'd give it a whirl with me.

I was always into Soul, the first record that ever hit me was the Contours – 'Do You Love Me', their version of that, which would have been in '63, when I was 12.

I started DJing in about '64 at Spenborough Youth Club. Then I did a cellar bar in Cleckheaton, the Hideaway, in about '68/'69. We didn't call it Northern Soul back then, we called it Uptown Soul. I used to go to Earlsheaton Youth Club in Dewsbury when Tony Banks played there on a Sunday night in about '70. We'd also go to the Bin Lid in Dewsbury, in about '68 , where I went to technical college. I'd go to the Ritz in Brighouse in the 60s for the rare Motown nights, and we'd go to a venue in Wakefield, the Metro, and I ended up DJing there in '71. I always bought and sold records. I went there one night with a box of records to sell and the DJ didn't turn up, so they said, "You've got a box of records, on you go." Around '69/'70, my mate Richard and I did a weekly Northern Soul night at the Coach and Six in Birstall.

I always loved the Central and do to this day. I've been to all the revivals bar the first one; they didn't know where I was, and I didn't know it was on. Paul Rowan tracked me down, and I've been to every one since.

I stopped going everywhere in '76. The music was changing, and I didn't like where it was going, plus I was getting married and starting a family. I got back into it in '95. I went on holiday on a canal boat and ended up in the Stoke-on-Trent area, and thought I'd go and have a look at where the Torch used to be. When I got home, I wondered what Keith Minshull was doing, as I'd been mates with Keith since the '70s. Eventually, I got in touch through his brother, and next thing I went to the Kings Hall all-nighter and that was it. I've been involved with the scene again ever since.

I'd do an early slot at the Central and then come back on later. In terms of records, I think I'm responsible for 'There's A Ghost In My House', although I'm not sure I'd want to admit that. It was an LP that didn't sell in '68, which I had a copy of, so I was playing it off that. I then got a 7" copy off Bradford market. I'd go there every week, saw a copy and thought nobody will know that; I'll have it. We'd go there every Saturday early afternoon, and you could pick stuff up four for a pound. Things you'd get there you could take straight down to the Torch and sell for a fiver, like Dottie Cambridge, all the MGM and Verve stuff, the Tymes and 'Walking The Duck', you could pick them up for 25p. I went with a lad called Richard. I did Spenborough Youth Club, and he did Thornhill Edge Youth Club, and we both worked for a mobile unit called Howard's Mobile Discotheque, he supplied all the rig, and we supplied the Soul and Motown.

There was no record player at the market stall, so you were buying blind. We'd buy anything that looked likely, but sometimes it was total rubbish. We'd take them back to my bedroom, where I had twin decks, and we agreed to alternate who would get the records off the pile, to keep it fair, unless someone ended up with something the other particularly wanted, and then we'd swap them. Richard used to collect white demos, and I am 100% convinced we had a [1]Frank Wilson there. Frank Wilson hadn't been discovered then, and it still hadn't been discovered in '76 when I dropped off the scene. Someone in '79 played it to me and

---

[1] *Frank Wilson – Do I Love You recently sold for £100,000, the sale facilitated by John Manship. The current owner has said he was immediately offered £125,000 for it for it, but turned it down. Frank Wilson went on to become a famous Motown producer. Berry Gordy, on discovering he'd cut the record, asked Frank if he wanted to be an artist or a producer, as he couldn't be both. He chose to be a producer and was told to scrap the copies of Do I Love You. The track was later covered by the white Motown artist Chris Clark. Frank Wilson died some years ago and never personally owned a copy, but by this point was aware of how collectable it had become in the U.K., in fact it was given legal British Tamla Motown release in the late '70s. Frank had become so famous on the U.K. Motown and Northern scene that he had a half page obituary in the Guardian when he died.*

said it was going to go massive. I said I've heard this before, I've had it, we got it off Bradford market. I said I haven't got it anymore, but that Richard must have it. He said you can't have done, there's only one copy in existence. I lost touch with Richard over the years, but I managed to track him down. He was working as a coach driver and I said, "Richard, you've got a record that is going to change your life." He knew exactly where I was going, but he said he hadn't got it, that I'd got it. He could remember it too. I've no idea where it went, but someone got very lucky. To be honest, it's still not one of my favourite records, and in the early days of Wigan anything Motown related wasn't considered to be Northern Soul, so my view is if I had ended up with it, I would have put it in my box to sell for a couple of quid.

Frank played more of the new Mecca stuff. We all used to go there, but in my mind, it wasn't Northern Soul. My top tunes in the day, all of which are now back in my box, were:

- Susan Barrett – What's It Gonna Be
- Eddie & Ernie – Can't Do It (which I broke while DJing at Wigan)
- Coasters – Crazy Baby
- United four – She's Putting You On
- Drifters – Got To Pay Your Dues
- Fuller brothers – Times A Wasting
- Eddie Holman – Eddie's My Name
- Marvellos – Somethings Burning
- Johnny Sales – I Can't Get Enough
- Dramatics – Inky Dinky
- Dottie Cambridge – Cry Your Eyes Out
- Hoagy Lands – The Next In Line
- Ambers – I Love You Baby
- Dee Dee Sharp – What Kind Of Lady
- Ethics – Standing In The Darkness
- Superlatives – I Still Love You
- Jimmy Soul Clarke – Sweet Darling
- Roy Hamilton – Cracking Up Over You

- Mary Love – Lay this burden down
- Fred Hughes – I Keep Trying
- George Blackwell – Can't Lose My Head
- Jackie Lee – Darkest Days
- Gene Chandler – Mr Big Shot
- Shane Martin – I Need You
- Pointer Sisters – Send Him Back (that's about as modern as I get)
- Billy Joe Royal – Hearts Desire

From '72 to '74 I'd drive from Huddersfield to Stoke-on-Trent every Tuesday, to get stock from Keith Minshull, to play or sell at the Central, Samantha's and Wigan. Frank said I had a copy of the Salvadors, although I have no recollection, but Keith Minshull found a box of 25 from that stall on Bradford market, so I suppose I might have had, but it hadn't gone big then. All my records went in about '80, and I had to start collecting again. I wasn't using them and thought I'd never use them again, plus I went through a divorce and needed the money. These days, everyone wants to be a DJ and is buying up all the records and driving prices up.

Frank and I did a club in Huddersfield called Taurus, and we had people like Kev Roberts and Richard Searling coming and playing for us. It was a bit of a dive but aren't all the best places. It was the worst place in Huddersfield, and there aren't any good ones. Frank and I went on to play at Wigan in the early days, '73, and he decided to stay on, and I didn't, which was probably a bad move on my part.

I'd sell records every week at the Central, and Pat Brady, who was a lot younger than me, would try and get into the Central for nothing, saying he was carrying my box for me. When I packed in at the Central, he saw an opportunity, and he started taking a box of records down every week, ultimately becoming a DJ there.

Frank's favourite record was the Carstairs, and when it was big in '74 everybody was after it, but you just couldn't get hold of a copy. Word got out that Frank had found a copy and was bringing it to the Central the following week. To try and get one up on him, I borrowed a copy off Keith Minshull, did a remix of it and cut an EMI disc, but a better version of it. Before Frank went on, I played mine! Later Frank took my remix to Tom Moulton (the famous Philly remixer) in the States as a concept, and Tom tidied it up and released a remix, which was obviously a far better version because he had all the gear.

Julian Bentley and I got our Emidisc machine in '74. We were cutting alternate mix tracks, speeded up or slowed down, album tracks on singles etc. We used to borrow ultra-rare stuff from Keith and make a few copies, and in return we would give him copies of stuff he didn't have. The strangest thing about that time is that I had an account with EMI who supplied us with blanks. What on earth did they think we were doing with them?

The Central got busted for drugs one night. I was there that night and got taken in with everyone else. The police stormed in, put the lights on and told everyone not to move. Anyone they thought was a likely suspect they took off. They took me, but I hadn't had any gear, but someone they found with gear on them said they'd got it from me, which they hadn't. The problem was I was still living at home with Mum and Dad, and my dad was unwell, he was on his way out. The police said if you put your hands up and admit to this, you'll just get a fine, but if you don't, we're going to turn your mum and dad's house over. I put my hands up, and as a result have a record for drugs, and actually I hadn't done them. I still can't go to the States even now, and this was '73. I can't remember who it was that gave them my name, which is a real shame as I could have exposed him in this book!

There was a bloke at the Central called Andy Simpson from Bradford. He had long, shoulder-length hair, which was very unusual on the Northern scene, and when he'd go into a spin, all the surrounding dancers got sprayed – you could see people backing away – he was like a shaking dog. When I went on, I always played stuff I knew he'd want to dance to, to see this spectacle.

The Central became part of a rota for us. We'd go there on Friday nights, then we'd go onto the nighter at Samantha's, try and get some sleep Saturday afternoon, then onto the Mecca Saturday night, and then onto Wigan, and then sometimes there'd be an all-dayer on Sunday. I don't know how we did it; I certainly couldn't do it now!

By '95 I literally only had a hand full of records left, I had nothing. I met up with Keith and started buying one or two. I got back into the DJ circuit by 2010, and I'd built up enough records to start playing again. I did Barnstable weekend, did Bridlington a couple of times, did Whitby, did the Torch revival, and then Paul Rowan rang me to tell me that the Central had started up again and they were looking for me. Steve Luigi's opening shot was, "I thought you'd died"!

One of the reasons I love the Central reunions is that its ethos was, certainly in the early days, that it played music that was actually played first time around. I tried to move it on a little, playing stuff that could have been played there if it had been known. Depending on who's DJing, it now plays a bit of everything. I focus on stuff made between '65 and '68, that's the core of what I like. Now they play R&B, which I've got into a little, but I don't fully understand it.

The Central, out of all the places I've been, has always been special. To be doing the same thing in the same place, often with the same bits of plastic going round, makes it all the more wonderful experience.

Ian Dewhirst's story, aka Frank:

The guys that got me into it were Sid, Smithy, Rob (who ended up running Sheridan's) – the Cleckheaton lot. I bumped into them when I was about 16 in '71 at a Soul night in Cleckheaton, I saw these lads with Torch badges on their blazers, and they took me under their wing. I also had a foot in the Huddersfield camp, and I bought my first collection from a guy who ran a clothes shop there called Lord Jim. He ran a Soul night at a club called Johnnie's and used to go the Wheel. I was sniffing out local Soul nights, but not quite old enough to get in the pubs and clubs. They told me about the Central. Leeds on a Friday night was a big night out. The Clecky lads took me along, but once I'd been there, I realised it was a cut above anything else I was going to.

I had been into mod and two-tone suits and all that stuff, style was always important to me, although I was still learning. When I got to the Central, I felt that buzz, and saw the way the guys danced and carried themselves, with that innate confidence that comes with being into Soul. The Central was the steep part of my learning curve; up to that point it had been youth clubs, but once I went down there, that was it, it became a Friday night fixture.

At the same time, I'm buying and selling records, and so I got to know Banksy pretty quickly, probably through pestering him to play tunes. I brought Earl Wright – 'Thumb A Ride' down one Friday, and he freaked out. Every week before I left, he'd say, "Are you going to bring your records down next week?" One Friday night, I was going on holiday the following week, and Banksy said, "Can you leave your records with me?" I didn't really like the sound of that, but I agreed anyway, on the condition he'd let me do the warm-up DJing when I got back. I came back and started playing between 9 and 10 o'clock on a Friday when there was hardly anybody in, then he'd come on at 10 o'clock and go all the way through to the end. That's the point when I really started collecting.

Friday nights were nine until one I think, but at 12 I'd be off to VaVa's or Sheffield Samantha's or places like that. I went down there in '71, '72. It was great for me doing the warm-up, along with Twink, who was from Liversidge near Cleckheaton and was also part of Clecky set. Twink was a collector as well, and he was well connected to Julian Bentley, who also lived in Liversedge. Julian was getting records from [2]Simon Soussan. Julian was about 5 years older than me, and was very much a Wheel boy and collector, and Twink's connection for getting good records. It was natural for Twink and I to get together, and between us we had enough records to get us through the night.

I don't quite know why Banksy left, because one minute he was there and the next he wasn't. I think he might have left in a bit of a strop, maybe with management. That's when me and Twink took over. I didn't speak to Tony again, he just disappeared, but he was also bootlegging records at the time. He bootlegged Jimmy Thomas – 'Beautiful Night', and I think he was coming to the end of his time and just moved on. I had a loud mouth and was doing a lot of gigs, so I was his natural successor. There was a time I was doing three gigs a night; I'd start at the Central, then go to Huddersfield Starlight and then onto to Sheffield Samantha's. I was also doing gigs through the week as well, so I was always a little bit livelier than the others.

I'd like to think I had a more professional style compared to most DJs on the scene at the time, and people tell me they could actually

---

[2] *Simon Soussan was born in Morocco and lived in Leeds before emigrating to Los Angeles. He was infamous on the Northern scene, as not only did he discover and send over lots of the early big sounds, he also bootlegged many of them, and as a result was very unpopular for a while. In addition, he produced versions of Northern Soul tracks and released them on his Soul Fox Records and Soul Galore labels.*

Soussan was also involved with the Frank Wilson 'Do I Love You' story. He befriended Tom DePierro at Motown Records, who had discovered one of the only two copies of the single in existence. According to Frank Wilson, the rest were destroyed after Berry Gordy gave him the choice of being an artist or a producer, where he chose the latter. Soussan allegedly acquired the copy from DePierro and made an acetate before selling it on. The acetate was a slightly sped-up version and was played under the cover up name of Eddie Foster, this version becoming the Wigan Casino classic. The original version was officially re-issued in the late 70s on UK Tamla Motown label.

hear what I was saying over the mic, perhaps because I was taught the Queen's English due to my southern parents! (laughs)

Before I got into the Northern, back in '66, '67, I was into Motown, and then started digging a bit deeper and tuning into Radio Luxemburg, listening on my transistor radio from under the pillow, when my parents thought I was asleep, and so I'd always like contemporary stuff. The term Northern Soul, contrary to what people say, was invented around '66, before Dave Godin coined the phrase. Record companies would call it the Northern Soul scene; I've got adverts from that time clearly stating the "Northern Soul sound".

I always thought I was about five years too young. I would have preferred to have been born in 1950, and then I'd have been right in the middle of it all in 1965, I'd have probably been down in London. We were lucky enough, though, to have been there at that point, to have heard about the Wheel and seen all the mods in town at the coffee shop, places like Lulu's, when we went shopping with our parents on a Saturday afternoon when I would have been 10 or 11. I was always pretty attuned to what was going on, reading about it and collecting records from '66 onwards. I knew there was a scene going on, I was just too young to be on it, but as soon as I got to 16, I ended up at the Central, and that was it.

I knew the Leeds guys, guys like Pete Dillon. Pete knows about the history of the Central; he had a few years on me, and he helped get me into it and build my knowledge. The Central for me was the heartbeat, and the introduction to the upper echelons of the Northern Soul scene.

I always liked the newer stuff. At that point I'd be going to the Central, but also Primo's on Saturday nights, where Paul Schofield was DJing. Paul is from Mirfield, and I'd bump into him at Mirfield Pentagon or places like that, where he was playing Funk, which I also liked.

I went to States in '76, so I think that's when I left the Central. I sold most of the records to fund the trip, and I brought Pat Brady in. I knew him from Central, he always wore a big leather coat, and I think it was me who took him down to Soul Bowl for the first time and introduced him to John Anderson. Me and Pat would go out record hunting together quite a lot.

When I came back from the States, I bumped into Paul, and he told me Primo's had finished. This was strange because it had always been packed, so I don't know what went on, but Paul said he was looking for another venue, and so we went down to see Len. At this point the Northern nights had fizzled out, and so that's when we set up the Jazz Funk nights, and the Central had its second wind.

We had some funny times down there. Do you remember Len would always give us a rendition on his organ of something or other on special nights, New Year's Eve and the like? I remember one night three drunks came in with a bad attitude, and one sat on his organ! He went fucking mad, that organ was his pride and joy, and in the end Fred Ward from Huddersfield had to sort them out.

It's hard to remember all the tunes, there were so many, but some of the records that meant a lot to me were things like Gil Scott-Heron 'The Bottle', 'Cochise' by Paul Humphrey, which was an immediate monster that nobody knew at the time and was a new release. The modern influence drifted in, records like 'Music Maker' by King Sporty, 'Seven Day Lover' by James Fountain, 'I Can See Him Loving You' by The Anderson Brothers, 'It Really Hurts Me Girl' by The Carstairs, which is my favourite record of all time.

If you look at the early disco stuff, like 'Free Man' by South Shore Commission, it was the same pace as Northern, but just a more modern recording. 'Super Ship' by George Benson; one of the biggest Northern records, even though it was a new release. Ian Levine had just got back from the States and I rang him on the Sunday to ask what he brought back. "The fucking biggest record

41

of all times, 'Super Ship' by George Benson." "What label's that on?" "A label called CTI. It's a new release in the States." Then I'd get the record, put it on, and yeah it all made sense. The scene hadn't yet split, but what you were getting was the newer stuff, things like 'You Sexy Sugar Plum' by Rodger Collins (which came from this fella in San Francisco, Bob Cataneo, "Disco Bob") but at the same time you'd still have things like Eula Cooper's 'Let Our Love Grow Higher', or 'No One Else Can Take Your Place' by The Inspirations.

The Esther Phillips 'What a Difference a Day Makes' was another one Levine brought back from New York, and I hammered it at the Central. These records coming from New York were new releases, but it was taking them six weeks to come through to England. Another example is' Love Factory' by Eloise Laws. A couple of dozen copies came through to the UK and that was it, it disappeared. Two or three years later, bang, it was massive. It didn't feel like it was rare, because it was on Music Merchant, and you used to see loads of crappy Music Merchant records, but not Eloise Laws of course.

Richard Searling's story:

Tony Banks was obviously an important DJ at the Central, and I had the pleasure of interviewing him on Jazz FM in '97/'98, and his knowledge was second to none: I didn't really need to ask him many questions, I just let him talk and talk he was that good. After many years in retirement, he'd made a "phoenix like" return to start the Brighouse all-nighter, and I think that's the reason we got him on the show. He spoke for over an hour about the clubs of West Yorkshire and his recall was unbelievable, a mine of information. I knew of him before then, but our paths had never really crossed DJing, because I think he'd essentially stopped just as I was really getting going, although he would occasionally phone me late at night, never before 11pm, because, apparently, he slept all day, but he would announce himself and then tell me all about a particular record or artist, at length.

I DJ'd at a couple of the Central all-nighters, which I think was in '73, with a lad called Rick Cooper. I remember because he played Audrey Slo – 'Gonna Find The Right Boy' on Swan, which I must have really wanted at the time, and Kent Meade – 'Funky To Me' on Magic Carpet, which remains obscure to this day. Fortunately, I wasn't at the one that got raided. I also did an all-dayer there at some point, which I remember due to an awful, violent incident that happened later in the day, with a chair being broken across someone's back! It must have been a Soul all-dayer, so quite why it all kicked off, I don't know. I don't remember there being any bouncers, so maybe some hooligans had just wandered down looking for trouble. They certainly found it.

My main venue was VaVa's at the time, and I hadn't yet moved on to Wigan, which started as a venue in late '73. I did a guest spot in October '73 and then started as resident in January '74. I don't actually remember Tony Banks being there at the Central, and I think I would have done because he was such a distinctive character. Ian Dewhirst, himself a larger-than-life character, was DJing with a box of 50, but with some great tunes in there; Linda Jones – 'Just Can't Live My Life', Delray's Incorporated – 'Destination Unknown' and Towanda Barnes – 'You Don't Mean It'.

Ian never seemed to have a lot of records with him, but always had great quality; if there was a record that had gone massive, he would do whatever it took to get it, even if it meant swapping half of his records to get the one he wanted. As soon as something got pressed or played out, he'd get rid of it and onto the next biggie, his taste was impeccable. Perhaps people like me were brought in because Tony Banks had left?

VaVa's was raided in July '73 and closed later that year, so it seems to fit that I DJ'd at the Central between VaVa's closing and me starting at Wigan. The Torch closed in February '73, so there was a real vacuum, which the Central filled. The scene was very much underground at that stage. I remember it being a small, compact club in a cellar, with steep steps leading down to it and pillars on the dancefloor, but it made for a great atmosphere and the place was rammed.

I can't remember with absolute certainty what I played those nights, after all it was a long time ago, but I'm pretty sure I would have played tunes that were big for me a VaVa's, things like the Adventures – 'Easy Baby' and The Volcanoes – 'Laws Of Love'. My wife, Judith, came with me, and I asked her about her recollections, but all she can remember is falling asleep, hopefully not during my spot!

Later that year, Brian Rigby and Alan Cain came up with the idea for Wigan and went to Jerry Marshall with the proposition they take over where the Torch had left off, despite the alternative version of events you may hear, and the rest is history. If the Torch hadn't closed, Wigan might not have happened: fate almost.

When I did the recent Solar Radio show on the Central, I got some fabulous letters, but there was one particularly memorable story, that Billy Bremner had once gone down there and asked for James Barnett – 'Keep On Talking' to be played. Not only an incredible player but with great taste in music. I really hope that's true.

Tony Banks recollections from the time:

Back in '63 I was playing things like Mel Torme – 'I'm Coming Home' and would you believe it, Motown, such as 'Please Operator' by Mary Wells, at the old Mecca in the County Arcade, '60 to '63, you'd be surprised what Soul music we used to play in those days, including a lot of Solomon Burke. Nowadays you get two to three hundred dancing, but in those days, it would be eight or nine hundred. I had a box full of British Sue demos from the early 60s, they were all brand-new releases, but its what's in the grooves that counts. I played tracks by artists you all know, but tracks you might not.

I did the original at the Locarno Bradford and some other Meccas dotted around the country. We had other clubs around West Yorkshire, The 3 Coins, that was a brilliant night, Earl Street Youth Club, that was very good, the Astoria Ballroom in Harehills, the Bee-Gee, Hernado's on Harehills lane and even the Esquire in Sheffield and Mr Stringfellow's Mojo; I used to spin a few times down there. Another place in Leeds was the good old Cro-Magnon, and of course the Spinning Disc. We were all spinning the same stuff, even a little club over in Manchester, whose name I forget, but it was something to do with a wheel.

Tunes from the time were:

- Solomon Burke – Cry To Me, Only Love Can Save Me Now (we played a lot of Solomon Burke)
- Mary Wells – Operator Operator (we were playing Motown even then, back in '63)
- Betty Everett – I've Got A Thing On You (R&B is raising its head again)
- Chuck Jackson – Any Day Now (we used to play all over the place, rarely hears these days because it's a bit slow for some people)
- Sammy Turner – Raincoat In The River (they used to jive around to this in the old Mecca)
- Homer Banks – A Lot Of Love
- Don Covay – Sookie, Sookie
- The Drifters – Baby What I Mean (a big sound at the Heartbeat)

The first three genuine Northern Soul beat type singles, before the phrase was coined, were:

- The Anglos – Incense (a 100mph, the first track with a fast Northern Soul type beat)
- Donnie Elbert – A Little Piece Of Leather
- Ad Libs – Appreciation (one we all know and something a little different, one we'd recognise as Northern Soul)

45

Everyone knows Dave Godin, but this one was on his other label, Deep Soul, an awful lilac colour, but little bits and pieces from the girls and the boys, the Ad Libs at their best.

Other clubs from the time were the String of Beads in Bradford, the Phonographic and the Bali Hai, and these were some of the biggies from those times:

- Vibrations – Dancing Danny (an old Chicago sound I've been playing since the 60s, a great sound and something a bit different)
- Earl Van Dyke – All For You (Motown from the early 60s, but that could still be played now, Intime specials)
- Little Hank – Mr. Bang Bang Man ('67 I used to play this a lot... but we're here for the music, not to listen to me spiel away)
- J. J. Barnes – Snowflakes (the sound of Memphis '69, brilliant, everyone knows this man, played at the Intime, that was a disco would you believe. Flip it over and you have a great B-side)
- Vernon Garrett – Angel Doll (another big Intime sound, on the Venture label)

Even in those days there was a lot of R&B played, way down underground at the Intime or upstairs at Hernando's, or at the Spinning Disc on the ground floor, or the Bali Hai, things like:

- Little Junior Parker – These Kind Of Blues (R&B from Texas, somewhere like Houston)
- Tony Clarke – The Entertainer (played at the Phonograph and String of Beads)
- Radiants – Voice Your Choice (also played at the String of Beads, Bradford)
- Impressions – Since I Lost The One I Love
- Dee Clark – Don't Walk Away From Me (I played this very early on in the 60s, down at the Intime, on would you believe the green Columbia label)

- Garnet Mimms – Looking For You (I've been playing this since '66)
- Major Lance – Investigate (very popular in '66, '67 and still being played today, I took it with me down to the Torch)
- Jackie Wilson – Nothing But Blue Skies (I used to play this upstairs at the Locarno, in the Bali Hai in Wakefield)
- Parliaments – Don't Be Sore At Me (another one that was popular at the Bali Hai on Mondays, Wednesdays and Saturdays. That's what launched me into Northern Soul, but it wasn't called Northern Soul, it was called Uptown Soul. That little man who passed away, Bub, used to come as a punter)
- Bobby Moore Williams – Baby I Need Your Love (another one from the Bali Hai, on the British Action label, Texas Soul)
- Fontella Bass – I Can't Rest (on the British Chess label, she's coming to rescue you)
- Joe Simon – The Girl's Alright With Me (let's move on, go a bit quicker, once again an English label, the Monument label)
- Gene Chandler – Fool For You (a nice little white piece of wax, with a nice big A on it)

In late '72, I flipped off to the USA, where I picked up one or two discs over there (about 15 tea chests full) including these, which I played at the Torch and Leeds Central:

- The Cavaliers – Hold On To My Baby (I found that in a warehouse in Brooklyn)
- Appolas – Mr Creator (good old Warner Brothers there)
- Billy Kennedy – This Is A Groovy Generation
- Big Dee Irwin – You Really Are Together (this was one of the ones I found in that little Brooklyn warehouse, the size of Lewis's, and before I found it, I don't think anyone knew about it)
- Rose Batiste – I Just Can't Leave You (more on the Thelma label, a little lady called RB, she's RB, I'm TB)
- Deon Jackson – That's What You Do To Me (a nice little white label)

- Jimmy Soul Clarke – If I Only Knew Then What I Know About You Now

Round about this time, Bali Hai, Torch, going to America, and of course the Central, '73, the golden years, these were one's that made the hairs on the back of your neck stand up and get your feet moving:

- Bobby Freeman – I'll Never Fall In Love Again
- The Charts – Desiree (there were actually two versions, would you believe, this one was the really thumping one, the other was a ballad)
- Garland Green – Girl I Love You (a big sound at the Central)
- Marjorie Black – One More Hurt

The Central was '73, and I also did a spot at the Torch after Major Lance, then we moved to the Intercom in Leeds, and it's around that time I made the famous trip to DJ at Wigan Casino, but never did, and so turned around and came straight back home. I did a few spots at the Wintergardens, where they tried to knock the pier into my head.

The Intime in those days wasn't a Soul club, but in actual fact it was, because all the people who loved Soul music always used to come down to the club, in the middle of Leeds, where we played things like:

- Barbara Lynn – You Left The Water Running
- The Astors – In The Twilight Zone (everyone knows Candy, but how many know this one)

Paul Rowan's story:

It's all a long time ago, but I do remember Richard Searling coming down to guest DJ and Alan Rhodes from York. Twink asked me to DJ originally, he was DJing with Frank at the time, but I started when Frank left. I bought records off Twink, that's how I got to know him; I'd go to his place almost every Sunday and our girlfriends at the time became close friends. This would have been around '75.

I'd been DJing for some time by this point, at Raquel's in Wakefield, Halifax Tiffanies, Annabella's in Harrogate, all-dayers and nighters for Terry Sampson, a local promoter. I was a well-established Northern DJ in West Yorkshire. Raquel's was my baby, I made it there, and Saturday nights were really big at the time and it was challenging the Central. Terry put on some good events, although never really premier league if I'm honest. He did the KGB all-nighter in Sheffield, which was a bit of a dump, but they were good nights. We also did the West Indian club in Huddersfield, which was OK for a while, but never really took off.

Twink made it clear he was looking to work with someone else. Frank was totally into the Mecca sounds, New York disco and Jazz Funk. He had stopped DJing at Wigan after getting flack for playing Bobby Franklin – Ladies Choice, which was too funky for Winstanley. That's when Frank started to DJ at Cleethorpes. I didn't mind the modern stuff but preferred the harder-edged Cleethorpes tunes, Black Nasty – 'Cut Your Motor Off' and East Coast Connection – 'Summer In The Parks', rather than the out and out disco.

There was a big split on the scene at the time, mainly precipitated by Ian Levine. To some extent I understand what he was doing, but to me it wasn't Northern Soul, he took it too far towards disco; there was no more Lou Ragland or Mel Britt. He was focused on bringing out his own productions, disco tunes such as the Exciters, LJ Johnson, Doomsday, they all had that tinkling xylophone in the background. Barbara Pennington and James Wells were the exceptions, great records. At the same time, he was playing brand-new tunes like Crown Heights Affair – 'Dreaming A Dream', which was too much for me, he'd stopped buying the rare tunes, it was simply lightweight New York disco. Forty years on as I look back, it was all good music, but at the time, it was such a diversion from traditional Northern Soul I struggled with it.

I was living in London at the time of the Central all-nighters when Tony Banks was around. He was a big influence and essentially mentored me, he taught me about Soul music. He was an acquired taste to many, but we always got along. I knew him from Wakefield Mecca, where he played Northern in one of the side rooms. This would have been around '71-'72. He would do the Mecca on a Monday night, and as I wasn't working, I'd often stay over at his and stay there until Wednesday, when he did another night down there. Everyone talks about Nev Wherry's British collection (who I DJ'd with at the Unity Hall at Wakefield), but it was not a patch on Tony's. He was a Mecca circuit DJ, and they were sent all the promos, the same as the BBC got. The rest of the mecca DJs weren't interested in Soul, particularly the more obscure stuff, so Tony got it all. They weren't interested in the Incredibles or Invitations or Little Anthony, they wanted Norman Greenwood – 'Spirit In The Sky', but Tony certainly was. He had everything on demos, Stateside and Tamla Motown, everything in consecutive order from 501 – 700s, including things that have since gone massive, Barbara McNair, Martha Reeves and the like, he had everything from its inception. He had all the Columbia, Philipps, Fontana, Polydor that got all the Ric-Tic stuff, United Artists, Sue, Cameo Parkway.

Before you got anywhere near Northern Soul with Tony, you had to sit down and listen to the Van Dykes – 'No man Is An Island', or the Impressions – 'I Love Silence', half an hour of the Ikettes, James Carr – 'Dark End Of The Street', deep Soul. I really appreciated the music and the education he was giving me. When he saw I appreciated it he took me under his wing, and we got on. I was welcome at his house and in the hallowed record room and was allowed to listen to what I wanted from his collection and make tapes. He let me DJ at Wakefield Mecca, doing the warm-up, where I started to learn the trade. I was always extrovert and had the confidence to pick up the mic.

Tony was his own man. He was older than us and a professional Mecca DJ, on the same footing as Saville. We were in our early 20s and he was in his mid-30s; it's not that he looked down on people, but he was almost a different generation. He wasn't interested in going to venues unless he was DJing, he felt the clubs needed him, not the other way around, and because of this, he may have seemed a bit aloof to some, but if you knew him, and he liked you, he was a gentleman.

Another time I went to his house I was telling him about Wigan and some of the stuff they were playing, for example Reperarta and the Delrons. He said, "Hang on a minute," and he got the stepladders out and disappeared up into the loft. Tony had this long, almost afro, ginger shoulder-length curly hair, but was as bald as a coot and had the most incredible combover. There was all this banging about, and next minute he's leaning headfirst from the loft, with this big mop of hair hanging down, brandishing a brand-new un-played demo in its birth sleeve of 'Panic'. He thought it was shite, hence the reason it was in the attic.

I took a job as assistant manager at Russel and Bromley, thinking it was in Leeds, which would have been great because my girlfriend at the time had just started at Leeds Carnegie, but it turned out to be in Manchester, and then they sent me to London. The last time I saw Tony was when I went up for the all-nighters, but it was just a brief "hello" because he was DJing, and he passed away shortly after. I think he had some kind of debilitating disease and ended up in a wheelchair. Tony Banks was the Central for me, the man had everything and put the Central on the Soul map.

Julian Bentley, a well-established Northern DJ, was also a mate of Tony Banks and had planned to go to America with him at the end of '72, prior to Tony starting at the Central. The trip was planned, but Julian had been naughty, and his visa application was declined. I was round at Tony's with Julian, and they were bartering over a copy of Rose Batiste – 'Hit And Run', which was really rare and in demand at the time. I asked how much, but Julian told me

I couldn't afford it; I was probably earning about £10 a week at that time, and he wanted £14. That's when it came out in conversation that Julian couldn't go on the US trip, but he said, "If I give you the money, will you go for me?" Unfortunately, I had to hold my hands up and confess I couldn't, as I'd been naughty too. Fortunately, based on Julian's experience, I never actually applied for a visa and I eventually went when the visa waiver scheme came. Julian was never able to go.

By this time, Tony already had everything that was being played at the Torch and the like on British, but when he came back from the US, he brought with him about 16 tea chests full of records, including Jimmy Thomas – 'Beautiful Night', that he had bootlegged out there. If you listen to these US pressed copies, it cuts off a few seconds at the beginning versus the British copies, because Tony's British demo that he copied it from had a chip out of it! He brought back stuff that has only recently come to light, things like Constellations – 'Didn't Know How To'.

When he died, I heard his wife had sold all his records to Gip Damone and Gary Fields, to pay to get central heating put in the house. Those records would have been worth hundreds of thousands now.

I DJ'd at Samantha's with John Vincent. Every now and then he would have a clear-out of records, and I picked them up; the Flirtations – 'Stronger Than Her Love', Yum-Yums – 'Big Thing', Sam Ward – 'Sister Lee', Maurice Williams – 'Being Without You', and these became big records for me at the Central. I'd buy about 10 records off John, but then have to work Samantha's oldies night for him for free for the next year to pay for them! Arthur Fenn also provided me with some of my bigger tunes. Arthur was a wheeler-dealer, he'd start the week with two records and then swap and barter for the next week at all of the venues and end up with five, the tunes the DJs wanted. You'd tell him what you wanted, for example Eula Cooper – 'Let Our Love Grow Higher', and he'd turn up with it a week later. He was big pals with Soul Sam, so had a great source.

There weren't many DJs put the work in I did, I worked five nights out of seven in local clubs, but then the all-nighters and dayers. As an example, Friday night I'd turn up at the Central, only to be met by Arthur telling me he wanted me to do a spot at the Manifesto in Selby, so I'd leave my girlfriend to play a box of records for an hour while I went to play there, then dash back to the Central, play until midnight and then dash over to Raquel's to play the last hour there, and then after to the Unity hall all-nighter, and then on to Cleethorpes on the Sunday! Eventually it burnt me out.

About a year after I started at the Central, Twink packed it in, and I was feeling a bit exposed. I asked Richard Searling to come and guest, which he did twice. There was a record that was getting a lot of hype but hadn't yet broken, Tony Middleton – 'Paris Blues', and Richard had a spare copy which he sold me, and I played it immediately on the Friday night. He then went on to play it at Wigan on Saturday, but arguably it was played at the Central first. I also played it on the Sunday at Cleethorpes, and Soul Sam said, "Oh, you're playing that now, are you?" The next Cleethorpes, Sam turned up with a copy; he'd always had it, but his was a rarer issue.

The crowd at the Central was a bit intimidating to be honest, there were still the original crowd down there, guys like Dave Maltas, Pete Dillon, Mick Eastwood, Steve Caesar. They'd been there from the days I started on the scene, guys I'd looked up to for years, so playing music to them felt a bit daunting; who was I to start playing to people who'd nurtured me in the first place? For that reason, it was always hard work because I felt they knew more than I did.

Towards the end, I had moved on from the traditional Northern and was playing what they might now term crossover; Bessie Banks – 'Don't You Worry Baby' (which I bought as a new release)

George Benson – 'On Broadway', Norma Jenkins – 'Can You Imagine That', Neighbours Complaint – 'Boogie In The Schoolyard'.

I'm enjoying the reunions, but they were tough for me initially because I had sold all my records; I had to borrow them off a friend of mine, who has a good collection, but I've built them back up now. I worked my set out for the first one, something I don't generally believe in because you don't really know how things will go down with the crowd, but I played my way through them, finishing with Gloria Jones – 'Come Go With Me', and it went down a storm.

The Central meant a lot to me then and still does now. There's no other club like it in terms of history and longevity, starting with Tony Banks, Twink, Frank, me, Pat, it always had quality headline DJs in residence, top records on the original labels. When dancers look over at the decks to see the record, they expect to see original vinyl, and they expect us to break new records. It was the local club that set the standard, much as Blackpool Mecca did on the other side of the Pennines; bear in mind neither were all-nighters (apart from the Central for a brief spell) and it represents Northern Soul in Yorkshire. It's iconic and enigmatic, it pre-dates Northern Soul from the mod days, there is nowhere else still going that can say that.

Robert Patricks's story, aka Swish

I was about 14 when I first went to the Central, in '67, before it was really a Soul club. I grew up in Leeds and was part of the Leeds scene around that time, Spinning Disc, the Intime, all those places. I really got into Soul when I heard the *This is Soul* LP in '68; it just blew my mind.

Before I DJ'd down at the Central, I was very active on the all-nighter scene, we'd travel all over, initially to the Wheel, and then Catacombs, Crewe, L'Ambassador in Bradford, Saint & Sinners in

Birmingham, VaVa in Bolton and the Torch. The Torch was incredible, and those tunes have stayed with me my whole life.

The people I remember from the early days are Eric Smith, who was the best dancer, Pete Dillon, Paul Widnall, Aidy Dundas, Sammy and too many more to mention. One infamous night I was dancing, and just before I went into a backdrop, I pushed my fist in the air, which was clad in a nice driving glove. It got stuck in the fan and ripped to shreds, leaving me in a heap on the floor, but giving all my mates hours of fun.

I started DJ'ing at the Central in about '73. By that time, I'd built a collection and Joan asked me to do the first and the last spot. I DJ'd with Paul Rowan and then later with Pat Brady. I was DJing on the very last night of the old Central and was on the decks when Len tried to wind it all up at the end of the night, but I wouldn't stop playing. Eventually he pulled the plug out, but the crowd kept chanting, "We want Swish, we want Swish"! A sad but memorable night.

Some of my favourite tunes from those days were:

- Mitch Ryder – You Get Your Kicks
- Round Robin – Kick That Little Foot
- Chuck Jackson – Good Things Come To Those Who Wait
- Roy Hamilton – Cracking Up Over You
- Duke Browner – Crying Over You

Great days that will stay with me forever.

I am writing my own book about these times, so all will be revealed.

Pat Brady's story:

I was going down to the Central in late '73 as a punter, and I can remember Tony Banks. It was always a great club and that was how it started for me. I heard later that Tony got into trouble with the Jimmy Thomas bootleg, and also had a crash in the States, but it's not really clear why he left. Frank took over when he did and started playing a lot of stuff that was played at the Mecca and Cleethorpes, progressive stuff. Frank got a copy of the Anderson Brothers; he had to swap about half of his box to get his hands on it. I was friendly with Frank and a Central regular at this point and had started to get into record collecting. I went down to Soul Bowl with him, I would have been about 16 at the time, and I also knew Twink from Samantha's in the early days.

As my collection grew, I soon became a full-time professional DJ. I was doing Halifax Digital on Monday with Graham Slater, places like the Peacock, various gigs in Lancashire, and Terry Sampson promotions, who was doing all-dayers in Doncaster and Sheffield with John Vincent, KGB all-nighters, and then the Ritz in Manchester, all over the country virtually.

Ian stopped DJing and was planning on going to the States, and he told Neil Rushton that I had good records, and as a result I got Ian's spot at the Ritz. I was becoming one of the top DJs, certainly the youngest top DJ, and had started to play the newer sounds, things like The Inspirations – 'Your Wish Is My Command'.

When Ian returned, he hooked up with Paul Schofield and started the Jazz Funk nights at the Central on Fridays, and the pair of them asked me to start a Northern night on Saturdays, it would have been around '78. Ian and Paul would buy all their Funk tracks together from Hunter at Jumbo; they'd go in there and he'd play them all the new stuff that was flooding in. I brought Swish in to join me for the Northern night because he had a lot of sway with the older crowd, and we had a few good years together there. I had a bit of a difference of opinion with Paul; I was being quite progressive and playing the new, rarer discoveries, which I thought was working as we were getting people in from all over the north, stuff like George Hobson, Rita and the Tiaras, Herb Ward – 'Strange Change', Chandlers – 'Love Makes Me Lonely', but Paul wanted me to play the more traditional Northern, which he felt the crowd wanted. Paul and Ian were billing the two nights as progressive Jazz Funk on Friday and traditional Northern on Saturday. They ran the venture as a business and paid me well, and for a while it was one of the hottest venues around. Len would come down from time to time, mainly for his personal enjoyment, despite being in his late 60s. He was a character and liked a drink, and his manager Joan was feisty to say the least, but it all gelled and we had great nights.

The Central was the start of my weekend DJing. I'd start there and then leave at around 12.30 to do the all-nighters, the KGB or somewhere like that.

People I remember are you and Jill (you always liked the rare stuff), Mally, Diane Layton, the York crew, Dave Law and Dave Ferguson from Lancashire, the Burnley lot, the Ward brothers, Dereck Noble, Kate, Steph, Diane Layton. So many faces it's hard to remember, and it was a long time ago.

I did my worst record deal ever down there with Dave Greet in about '77. I had a spare of Billy Woods, which I'd been playing as an oldie at the Ritz, and foolishly I swapped it for a copy of Rita & The Tiaras, I wanted it that much. Hindsight is 20:20.

I still enjoy DJing, but I have the record and promotions business and have nothing to prove, I'm very comfortable with my life, with my three children doing well, and I've become a grandad this year.

Some of my top tunes from those Central days, many of which I covered up to protect their uniqueness and throw others off the trail, were:

- Walter & Admirations – Life Of Tears – La-Cindy
- Frank Dell – He Broke Your Game Wide Open – Valise (covered up as Bobby Franklin)

- Chandlers – Your Love Makes Me Lonely – Col-Soul (courtesy of the late Andy Riding)
- Gene Toones – What More Do You Want – Simco WD
- Rita & Tiaras – Gone With The Wind – Dore D
- General Assembly – Sensitive Mind – Desiree (covered up as Don Varners soul generation)
- Herg Ward – Strange Change – Argo D (covered up as Sam Williams)
- The Construction – Hey Little Way Out Girl – Sync 6 (covered up as Del Capris)
- George Hobson – Let It Be Real – Sound City
- Aspirations – You Left Me – Peaches
- Dean Courtney – Love You Just Can't Walk Away – MGM D
- Pat Lewis – No One To Love – Solid Hit (covered up as Eula Cooper)
- Billy Hambric – She Said Goodbye – Drum (covered up as Steve Mancha)
- Danny Woods – You Had Me Fooled – Correc-tone
- Melvin Davis – Find A Quiet Place – Wheel City
- Inspirations – Your Wish Is My Command – Midas
- J.C. Messina – Time Won't Let Me – Tom King Productions (covered up as Bob Seger System)
- Purple Mundi – Stop Hurting Me Baby – Cat (covered up as George Blackwell)
- Bobby Womack – Find Me Somebody – Atlantic (covered up as Lenny Curtis)
- Wilbur Walton Junior – 24 hours Of Loneliness – 1-2-3 D (covered as Sammy Campbell)

CHAPTER 6

THE DANCERS

Having heard the story from the DJ's perspective, now it's time to hear from the dancers, the ones who literally brought the club to life and created its unique culture and atmosphere. I wanted to capture the stories authentically in their own style, later seeking out the common experiences that bond us together in that moment in time.

Some people have both DJ'd and danced, guys like Chris Mallows, Rick Cooper, and Steve Luigi, but I've put them in what I believe to be their section of best fit, dancers first and foremost.

Several of the DJs mentioned the name Pete Dillon from the early days and asked if I'd talked to him. I didn't know Pete at the time, so I tracked him down and caught up with him for his story, he was the starting point.

Pete Dillon's story:

In '67 to '68 it was a "beat" club, with a mixed crowd dancing to the music of the day. I started going in '68 when it played more commercial Soul. Before the mods took over, it had been a bit of a rocker club due to the close proximity to the Star & Garter and the Whip. In early '69 there were mass brawls, until eventually the rockers stopped coming because they were getting battered every week.

I was a bit too young to claim to be one of the Bee-Gee crowd, but then in '69 a mod coffee bar just off Boar Lane called the Conk, changed its name to Lulu's. It had a cellar bar and club downstairs, and we started going there. It was pretty seedy and has since become infamous. There used to be a Chinese guy down there with long hair and a long leather coat, who had a samurai sword strapped to his leg! There was a hard core of 25–30 regulars, hard lads, and I used to think, *thank god I'm on their side*. There were mods, skinheads, suedeheads and West Indians, a right mixture as it should be, and how it was in the 60s, everyone together, there was never any racial tension at all. We became known as the Lulu's and got into some famous battles around Leeds with rivals, but that's another story. Lulu's were instrumental in the Central rocker brawls too. Elsewhere in Leeds, the last year or so of the Old Mecca was home ground to a mixture of Bee-Gee, Lulu's, West Indians and a proper cross-section of townies.

The Lulu's crowd who were into the music like me, went to the Central as well. The man on the door at the time was a black guy called Willie Richardson, who was famous and later became Mr Universe, along with his brother Tony. The club was renowned for being a bit rough and ready. A lot of the older mods from that time were from Chapel Allerton and Moortown, and they thought the Central was a bit rough, and so they started going to the New Mecca after the Old Mecca closed, but we were from the other side of town and felt at home.

In 1970 the Bee-Gee had closed, and all the older lads who'd gone to the Wheel started coming to the Central on a regular basis. They brought their tunes down and we used to coerce the DJs to play them. The DJs at the time were people like Denis Billingham, Andy Harrison, Dave Smith, Malc Burton and others. I think Denis may have DJ'd in the 60s. Between us, we all used to do a bit, we all took a box down and it was very informal. Running alongside the Central at that point was the Metro in Wakefield, but that too got raided.

A couple of lads, Denis Billingham and Mick Eastwood, decided to open a club in Harehills, at a place called Hernando's, which had been a long-standing club above a café. They rechristened it

Hernie's and we put two or three all-nighters on. I had a job serving espresso in the coffee bar, but then that got raided. In the meantime, Joan, the manager at the Central, decided we were banned from the club for putting on a rival night, and so we didn't go for about six months and travelled to clubs in other towns. When we went back, all was forgiven, but things had really started to take off and by that time Tony Banks, Keith Atkinson and Tony Jackson were there, which was around '72. It was open Friday and occasionally Sunday then, and we'd go back down on Sunday, having been wherever to an all-nighter.

Keith and Tony Jackson are still DJing at the all-dayers. I'd bump into Keith every Friday in Jumbo Records; he would buy all new releases and whatever imports they had. This was in the early '70s. He told me recently he has never sold a record.

Tony Banks had been a Mecca DJ, he did Wakefield Mecca, and I think he'd done some radio. He was a lot older than any of us and had an amazing record collection. I once went to where he lived, his mum's house, and going into his backroom, which was about 12' square and lined floor to ceiling with singles on every wall. You'd mention a record, say O Jay's – 'I Dig Your Act', and he'd pull out a UK issue, UK demo and an import copy. He had everything, but he still wouldn't sell you one! He'd done well and went to the States and got a load of stuff, which took off at the Torch. He used to take me down to the Torch to sell his pressings on TB super soul.

At some point Tony left, and Ian Dewhirst and Twink took over. Ian said we used to frighten him to death, these older guys looking at him and critiquing what he was playing. Pat Brady also DJ'd in the mid-'70s.

I missed the notorious raid at the Central, in fact I missed two of the three raids at Yorkshire Soul clubs, the other being the Metro. People wondered how I'd done that, but it was sheer good luck I can assure you.

It's difficult to remember specific Central tunes, and of course many of them had been played at the Wheel or Torch, but there were great new releases around, things like Millie Jackson – 'My Man Is A Sweet Man', and Timothy Wilson. Around this time, we discovered the record stalls in Leeds and Bradford market were full of great tunes for next to nothing. They fed the collectors and DJs for a long time, the older stuff like Jackie Lee – 'Darkest Days' and Eddie Parker – 'Love You Baby'. We used to go to VaVa's in Bolton, another seedy club, where Richard Searling was resident DJ. A lot of the stuff that's gets credited to Wigan was actually played by Richard down there, stuff like Moses Smith – 'Girl Across The Street' and Otis Smith – 'Let Her Go', and once the Central DJs got copies, they were played there too.

Chris Mallows and Dave Maltas were some of my closest friends from the time; we'd go to the Torch together, and Chris did a bit of DJing down at the Central and does all the reunions. He is a brilliant DJ and still, in my opinion, the best there now.

The all-nighters started around '73, but they stopped when it got raided. I went to most of them, but one night I was stood in the doorway having a chat when some lads I knew from the Leeds games approached me, all notorious hooligans and nut jobs. One of them said, "We've heard there's a load of Manchester here and were going to have 'em." I said, "No, they're not football fans, they're nothing to do with football, it's a Soul all-night, there's people from all over, Liverpool, Sheffield." Their eyes lit up even more, but luckily, I managed to defuse the situation and persuade them to leave it, and off they walked, muttering to themselves, no doubt to get their kicks somewhere else.

There were always funny incidents there that have stuck in my memory. Swish used to wear leather racing gloves, as many of us did, and one night he was dancing away and stuck his hand up to go into a backdrop and got his hand caught in the ceiling fans! It ripped his glove to shreds.

Another notable story was when I organised a party at mine one night. I was still living at home then, and I invited Dave Godin. I used to write to Dave a lot: he was a big letter writer, some of it about music, but also about his challenge of the censorship laws. The idea was we'd have the party and then go down the Central. Amazingly, Dave turned up, but by the time we were ready for the Central, Dave had got tired and wanted to go to sleep. I had to stay with him, but everyone down the Central was talking about him being in Leeds, not knowing at the time he was asleep at my mum and dad's. I've got a photo of him in my mum's kitchen.

On another night the doors were locked, with the club absolutely rammed. All of a sudden it was even more rammed; people were pouring out of the ladies' toilets after scrambling in through a small window! The dancefloor was standing only, no room to dance, we were like sardines.

The Central meant everything to me at the time. I could have been laid up in bed for days with flu, but come the Central night I was up, even if I was dying. It was our way of life. It was the most important venue at that moment in time because it kept the scene going after the Wheel and the Torch had been forced to shut their doors.

Martyn Ellis the Torch DJ turned up one all-nighter and ended up doing a spot, it was a lot more flexible in those days. When it was open Fridays in the early-mid 70s, we used it as a starting point for the weekend, some going to Wigan, VaVa's, Blackpool Mecca or Samantha's at Sheffield. The Central really doesn't get the credit it deserves. For a few years in the late 60s, it was our hometown club, then for a few more in the 70s it attracted all the big faces on the scene along with the DJs on their nights off. I stood at the door one night and watched Alan Day, Martyn Ellis and Ian Levine walk in. I thought at the time *this club has arrived*!

Pete's top Central 45's

- Jackie Lee – Darkest Days
- The O'Jays – I Dig Your Act
- Moses Smith – Girl Across the Street
- Otis Smith – Let Her Go
- Eddie Wilson – Toast To The Lady
- Gladys Knight & Pips – Just Walk In My Shoe
- Tony Middleton – My Home Town
- Ruben Wright – I'm Walking Out On You
- Timothy Wilson – Love Is Like An Itching In My Heart
- Billy Harner – What About The Music
- Velvelettes – These Things Will Keep Me Loving You

Derek T Barnett's story:

My salon on Great George Street in the mid-'60s, Character Hairdressing, was very popular. Myself, Daz and Peter Cornelius cut all the mods' hair. I played Tamla Motown all day long in the shop. It was suggested I make promotional posters for the shop, calling myself Derek "Tamla" Barnett, so I got someone to print them up, except he got it wrong, and it came out "Tamala". The name stuck and from that point I was Derek Tamala Barnett, or DTB. We later moved to the balcony in the Queens Arcade, near to Jumbo.

On Saturdays, there would be loads of scooters lined up outside the original shop. I never had one personally, but I had a nice red convertible Triumph Herald, which added to my popularity. Working at Lewis's in '63, I'd go down to the old Mecca at lunchtime, where Mick Sheard was one of the resident DJs. I met Daz there and our lifelong friendship developed, we were like brothers.

I was probably the first guy on the Soul scene to ever walk down the Central steps, as I went to Len Cave's school of dancing to learn to ballroom dance. On Saturdays, Len had a Beat music night, but then around '65 it became more groups and Soul music. I can remember going to one of the first Soul do's there with Bernard Finnell (probably the first mod in Leeds), Mick Sheard and Daz, the originals. Around '65/'66 my mates Colin Vernon and Pete Hardwick DJ'd, then followed by Tony Banks, Keith Atkinson, Twink, Frank, Swish and Paul Rowan.

At the same time, we were all going to places like the Cro-Magnon, the Three Coins, the Blue Gardenia and the old Mecca. Contrary to the stories, Tony Banks had all the tunes before everyone else, he had everything, typically on British and import, he was a legend.

I first went to the Wheel in '64, when it was on Brazennose Street, where I saw acts such as Brian Auger, Long John Baldry and Spencer Davis when he was a very young lad. In September '65 it moved to Whitworth Street, and they started getting the black American Soul artists across, most of whom I saw: Edwin Starr, Inez & Charlie Fox, Ike & Tina Turner and more. Much later I also went to the Torch, but probably only about five times, the Wheel was my place.

Records from those times, still played today, included Fats Domino – 'It Keeps Rainin' (which was often the last record played at the nighters and brought many a tear to my eye) Darrell Banks – 'Open The Door To Your Heart', Hoagy Lands – 'The Next In Line', O' Jays – 'I Dig Your Act', Gloria Jones – 'Finders Keepers', Homer Banks – '60 Minutes Of Your Love', Incredibles – 'Nothing Else To Say Baby'. They call it Northern now, but back then it was just Soul, Uptown Soul, until Dave Godin renamed it.

I went to the first Central all-nighter circa '69, long before the ones in '73, by which time I'd stopped going as much. I met Margaret in '74, we married some years later and have been together ever since.

It's great what Steve Luigi has done to get it all back together, and hopefully we'll all be back there soon. All the people from those early Central days, I loved them then, and I love them now.

Malc Burton's story:

I worked on the corner of Briggate and Boar lane and used to go to the lunchtime dos at the old Mecca, the Spinning Disc, and I'd always be late back. At the time there were few places playing Soul music, and I heard about the Central via word of mouth. I started going down there at the beginning of '67 and was also going to the Wheel and other venues. It became a regular haunt, but in the beginning, it had a hardcore Rock 'n' Roll fraternity; however it gradually changed to Soul. A lot of people have rose-tinted memories of those days, but it wasn't like that, it was rough! I was talking to a girl down there one night and her boyfriend got a bit upset and hit me with his crash helmet.

Tuesday nights were pretty spartan, but it was a good meeting place. One bank holiday, in '68, the DJs who were supposed to be on didn't turn up, so Joan asked me to play a few tunes until they got there, which they never did. At that time, the Central had their own record collection, with "The Central School of Dancing" stamped on them, so I just played them. We started playing some of the Motown and Stax stuff and the club slowly transitioned. This was before the days of Andy and John. I remember Andy had a really nice scooter and then progressed to a white convertible Triumph Herald, which tended to attract members of the opposite sex. These were the days when Bill Richardson was on the door, whose favourite group at the time was the Ventures, the guitar group, and he'd bring an album down for us to play, a request you weren't going to decline. There was a variety of music played, including, R&B, Ska and Bluebeat.

Some of my favourites from those early years were Rex Garvin – 'Sock It To Em JB', Bob & Earl – 'Harlem Shuffle', Howlin Wolf – ''Smokestack Lightening, and some of the Bo Didley stuff.

I left Leeds in the summer of '68 and was going all over the place, something I regret now, and only returned at the time of the all-nighters, the Tony Banks days in '73. Fortunately, I wasn't there the night of the bust; I'd already had my wrists slapped in Stoke in '72, so I was very wary.

The Central was one of the hottest venues on the scene at that time, it was unbelievable, and it was great to see Steve Luigi organise the revivals. The first one was the first time I'd been in the club since the all-nighters. It was a surreal experience. I was a little disorientated at first, it had been so long, in a venue I was very familiar with; I'd ended up decorating it twice in the late '60s, emulsioning it. It always felt a bit weird down there when you were on your own, the toilets were particularly creepy. Len was always a cheapskate, but I'd do anything for Joan; I did it on my days off, free of charge.

Later I started Wakefield Unity all-nighters in '76 – '77, that's where I gave Pat his first all-nighter, but unfortunately someone nicked his full-length leather coat at one of them. I've kept promoting and doing various things over the years ever since.

Looking back, I knew I loved the music, but the Central was the catalyst that brought it all together for me.

Dave Maltas's story:

My first recollections of Soul were from about '66. I went to a youth club on a Sunday night called St Antony's, which played tunes such as 'The Entertainer' by Tony Clark, a super cool record which made me aware there was more to music than the pop beat combos in the charts. From there we started going to the Spinning Disc, which was in the County Arcade, where Reece is now. This was around '67; they had Ben E King and many others on there. There'd be lines of scooters parked outside, and wall-to-wall mohair suits. I was spending time hanging out in coffee bars most nights, feeding the jukebox so I could hear the likes of Tightrope. Walking round with the *Impressions* LP under your arm, listening and dancing to all the Stax, Atlantic and Motown new releases, and going to things like the Stax/Atlantic review and thinking *it will never get any better than this...* but it did.

I first went to the Central around '68, but it wasn't a Soul club as such then. It was one of those places where people would say you don't want to go there, it's a dive, it's a den of iniquity, but perversely that's what drew me to it. They played some Soul music, but they also played Rock 'n' Roll and the pop tunes of the day. Willie Richardson was the doorman. In those days there were two types of membership card; those for over 18 and those under, because of the bar. One of Willy's tests as to which category you went into was to grab hold of you by where your sideboards should be, and if there was nothing there to pull, he'd tell you no, you're under 18.

The Saturday nights were still ballroom dancing. They opened the modern music nights on Friday, Sunday and Wednesday. Joan and Derek ran it, and Len Cave was the owner. I initially went down with guys from my home turf in Beeston, but in '69 I bought a scooter, even though the mod scene had all but ended in Leeds, and by that time the Spinning had closed. We formed a scooter club called the Haig, later to become the Inca's, which had quite a reputation around Leeds. Around this time there were endless fights at the Central, mostly fronted by the Lulu's lads, who hung around in a café of the same name. Eventually all of the remaining rockers were kicked out, and the Central became ours. Some of the older lads started to play predominantly Soul music, records they'd heard at the Wheel and had in their collections. Andy Harrison, aka Scotch Andy, was one of the main DJs. He was a regular at the Wheel with guys like Mike Eastwood and Denis Billingham, up to when it got closed down in '71. The Metro in Wakefield and Hernie's in Leeds, which was run by Mike and Dennis, then opened for all-nighters. Joan actually banned them both from the Central for running a rival club, but I'm not sure if she ever told them directly. Hernie's got raided and shut down after a few nights, along with the Metro, and so the Central became the number one Soul club in the Leeds area, and the place to be.

Some of the older guys started to get married and leave the scene, and I picked up quite a number of their records. By this time Keith Atkinson was DJing with Tony Jackson at the Central. Tony Banks was on all the mailing lists, Motown and the like, and came originally as a guest DJ. He had all the British demos from the record companies and an incredible collection, ultimately becoming the main DJ.

The Torch opened in '72, and we'd pick records up there and bring them back to the Central, which was now 100% Northern Soul. We also had Jumbo Records on the balcony in the Queens Arcade, and Bostock's Records in the Merrion Centre, where they had thousands of US imports. We were buying a lot of stuff on MGM and Verve, picking them up for next to nothing. This all added to the reputation of the Central as being one of the top clubs in the north. Rick Cooper, who was at Leeds University at the time, had now joined the DJ roster, as well as Chris Mallows, Twink, Frank and Steve Luigi.

When the Torch closed, there were no all-nighters anywhere, except for the short-lived VaVa's in Bolton. That's when we persuaded Joan to have an all-nighter in '73. I went to most of them, except the infamous one that got raided. We'd gone somewhere else that night, because part of the all-nighter experience for me was not only the music and the people but the adventure of going to a strange far-off town. Some of the magic was lost when all you had to do was jump on the number 52 bus.

It's strange, but I can always spot people from the Central by the way they dance. It's more dancing on the spot, mainly because there was no room to move. Eric Smith and Steve Caesar were both top dancers, along with Matchy from Rotherham, who won the dance competition at the Torch.

Dave Godin came through one night to a party Pete Dillon was holding, but I don't think he actually made it down to the Central for some reason. There was a lot of anticipation at the Central he was coming.

My wife was a tailoress, and she'd make suits for many of the people down there, guys like Eric Smith. They'd try them on in the toilets, which was a bit like trying one on in a phone box, and they'd walk out to the bar area, and she'd be down on her hands and knees, pinning their trousers up. Now that's what I call service.

There are certain records always remind me of the Central, because they were played almost exclusively down there, and then others that just remind me of the Central but had actually been played at other venues. From the early days these included:

- Bobby Wells – Let's Copp A Groove
- PP Arnold – Everything's Gonna Be Alright
- Sam Nesbit – Black Mother Goose
- Lorenzo Manley – Swoop Down On You
- Sonny Charles – Black Pearl
- Clifford Curry – Can't Get A Hold Of Myself
- Chubby Checker – Black Cloud
- Zoot Money's Big Roll Band –Big Time Operator
- Dee Dee Warwick-We're Doing fine

Our crowd included Sue, Chris Mallows (who I met through scooters and persuaded him to come down) Lesley, Pete Dillon, Dave Thompson, Anne, Colin Vernon, Ian Smart, Charlie Fineberg, Steve Goodison, Roy Adams, Julie Tate, Tony Jackson, Cheryl and Paul, Steve Luigi, Spud, Bev, Swish, Eric Smith, Al Stevenson, Rob Hirst and many more.

The Central was a massive part of my life and everything revolved around it. We'd meet there on the Friday, and also later when it opened on Saturdays, and then be off to the all-nighters at Wigan and Cleethorpes and all-dayers for the rest of the weekend, then back to the Central on Sunday and Wednesday evening. We were into a broad spectrum of Soul music, not just what they now call Northern, and it was, and still is, the core of my life. The songs are a like a time capsule, instantly taking you back for two or three minutes, when you are lost and forget whatever shit may be going on in the rest of the world, when the music completely envelopes you so deeply you care for nothing else.

I go to most of the reunions, but the one I like most is the Christmas one because it takes me right back: everyone up on the streets running around like headless chickens doing their shopping, with us dancing obliviously down below in our own cool and secret world.

Chris Mallow's story:

The phrase "Northern Soul, a way of life" is a bit of a cliché I guess, but for me like most of us, it really has been, although in '69 we didn't call it Northern Soul. If I remember rightly, we nicknamed it Uptown Soul because we went up town to listen to it.

For some unknown reason, when I turned 16, I decided I wanted a scooter, although I knew bugger all about Lambrettas and Vespas and my mates at the time were buying motorbikes. Maybe it was fuelled by the girls at school ganging up on people asking, "Are you a mod or rocker?" or maybe it was a guy around our way who had one, although I didn't like the look of him; he seemed a right cocky, big-headed git! This turned out to be Dave Maltas.

I was coming out of a petrol station one day, and this lad went past on a scooter, who recognised me from school, Andy Birkhead. He never got into Soul, he couldn't understand guys dancing on their own, but he invited me round to his house to meet some of his mates, who were in the Haig Scooter Club. When I got there, the cocky lad's scooter was parked outside, and my heart sank. Dave has since made amends and became my best mate and was best man at my wedding. I call it destiny.

The rest of the group kept telling me about this club they went to and wanting me to go with them, but me not being that confident back then, and still a bit of a div, I kept putting it off. I just didn't know what to expect, as I'd never even done the youth club thing, so going to a proper night club was a bit daunting. I was sat at home one Friday evening, feeling left out like an idiot, and I thought, *sod it, I'm going to go*. I got dressed and got my arse down there, and after that, I never looked back. Buying a scooter and going to Leeds Central changed my life.

The Central was still a ballroom dancing school at the time, but had "beat" nights on Tuesday, Friday and Sunday, playing the tunes of the day from the likes of Motown, Stax and Atlantic. I had no real idea what I was listening to, or why I loved it so much, but it turns out it's not called Soul music for nothing, and I caught the bug. This was about '69 to '70. The club was essentially a mod club and had taken over from the Bee-Gee, which by this time had closed. The DJ was Andy Harrison, aka Scotch Andy. I'd always nag him to play Round Robin – 'Kick That Little Foot Sally Ann'. One thing I'll never forget was when Scotch Andy asked if I wanted tickets to see Jackie Wilson. I innocently replied, "Who's she?" What a div, how little did I know.

I met some great people and firm friends down those magical Central stairs; Dave Maltas, Mike Eastwood, Pete Dillon, Keith Atkinson, Tony Jackson, Kevin Barret, and most importantly my then girlfriend and future wife, Lesley, who I first met at Wakefield Intercon and who ended working behind the bar at the Central.

The Central has been a massive part of my life. We had a really tightknit group of mates who went all over to various events, but always returned to the Central, our spiritual home. After a while the numbers started to drop off, and three nights became two, and there was genuine talk of the club closing. At the same time, we spotted an advert in *Blues & Soul* magazine for an all-nighter at a club in Stoke-on-Trent called the Golden Torch. Enquiries were made through Jumbo Records, a great hangout out for all us cool kids.

So, on the night we dressed up to the nines, got on a coach in Leeds, and headed off to this foreign land; it was like another world. Wow, what an experience that was! As soon as you walked through the doors, the atmosphere hit you like brick, and it was like being on another planet. I thought I knew a bit of Soul music by then, but not a chance, they played three records all night that I knew, and the rest were just awesome. There were some incredible dancers there, guys like Frank Buper, doing "Arab springs" and spinning into backdrops.

After a night out at the Torch, we'd return to the Central on Sunday night, trying to copy the moves, spinning but falling over. Joan (who remember was a ballroom dance instructor) came over and asked what we were trying to do? We explained and she said, "Keep your head straight." I always remembered that and it worked, from that point I was brilliant at spinning! There was another good spinner at the Central, I think he was called Fizz from Barnsley, and we'd always kind of battle in a friendly way. All this has led to quite a few adventures, and gradually I really go into the music and dancing, which has always been a big part of it for me, once I learned I didn't have two left feet that is.

Scotch Andy moved on, and a couple of the crowd, Keith Atkinson and Tony Jackson, took over the DJing, having built good record collections of their own. I'd built a collection of around 50 records in a box, and I'd take them down and do the early warm-up spot. This would be around '71-'72, and word was getting out about this great little club with a fantastic atmosphere, and its reputation grew and grew. It became one the most iconic clubs on the scene, and still is, having allowed a few big-name DJs to cut their teeth behind the decks.

Tony Banks was brought in for the monthly all-nighters in '73 on Saturday nights, originally as guest DJ, but then becoming resident. We really didn't have enough of the big tunes which were beginning to emerge, and TB had them. Pete Dillon knew him, and he really knew his stuff; I think he was making trips to the US and bringing stuff back, as well as all the demos he got from the record companies.

I liked to play stuff that was a bit different, things like Don Browning – 'Dream World', Major Lance – 'Um, Um, Um, Ain't No Soul' and some of the Torch stuff, 'Quitter Never Wins', 'Too Late', 'Shing a Ling', 'Purple Haze', 'Kick That Little Foot', 'Devil In A Redress', 'Breakout'. I saw Major Lance seven times, including the Torch. He was the first Soul star I ever saw, at Tiffs in Halifax the first time. Me, Dave and Pete also saw him at the Hypnotic in York, but there was a bomb scare halfway through. We were all outside and we managed to have a chat with him. He remains one of my favourite artists of all time.

Me and Lesley were there the night the Central got raided, but I'd been a good boy and didn't get arrested. They searched my bag and asked where my car was, but I said I didn't have one, it was a scooter parked in the dark arches near the station. When they'd carted everyone off, they left a couple of police cadets to keep an eye on us, and we were allowed to put the music back on. Ian Dewhirst played Garnet Mimms – 'Looking For You', I assume tongue in cheek, and everyone was pissing themselves. There were a lot of arrests, but I don't think there were many convictions.

Another big adventure came in 1973 when I was approached by two young scooter boys who I had briefly met the year before. They asked if I would be interested in forming a new scooter club, as I was the only one of the original crowd who still had one. I jumped at the chance, as I'd really missed it. That was the start of something big, the birth of the biggest club in Leeds, and remains so to this day.

After much deliberation about a name, it was suggested we use the name of club we all loved, and thus the Leeds Central Scooter Club was born. It became an iconic road club and race team, which I have been very proud and privileged to have been a part of over the years, just as I am the of Soul club that preceded it.

I got married to Lesley in '76, and most of the guests were from the Central, including Joan and Derek, the managers. I'd got into scooter racing, and so I was away quite a lot of weekends, and stopped going quite as much, as the music was beginning to cross over. Steve Luigi, Fred Ward and Pat Brady were DJing in that final phase.

The Central meant everything to me at the time. The kids came along, and I had to slow down towards the end, but if it hadn't been for the Central, I wouldn't have met Lesley and there'd have been no kids.

The club eventually closed its hallowed doors in the mid-eighties but remained a music venue in various guises, rock, pop and punk until a certain small person got in touch with the management of the now HiFi Club, explained the history of the place, and asked about staging a one-off reunion all-dayer, a one-off that has now been running for seven years. They knew some of the history and were delighted to support the idea, and I'm so happy to be part of the DJ line up and the whole thing.

Mike Eastwoods's story:

1967 I'm 16 years old and at the grammar school, and the mates I knocked around with in Headingley weren't really into the mod thing. I'd seen all the stuff about mods on the telly from way back to '63 and was always attracted to it, but I didn't actually know any. There were a couple of lads at school who were kind of into it, but the grammar school was mainly middle class, and these youth cults tended to be more working class, so I wasn't really in the right environment.

A mate of mine, Ian Rogers, got a Vespa scooter from Marsdens at Hyde Park, and we started talking about the mod scene. By '67 we were going into town to the old Mecca. I was still at school and a "server" to the younger kids on my table at lunch, which allowed me to sneak out once I'd hurriedly dished out the grub, and go to the Mecca for half an hour or so. You soon got to know people and get familiar with the club Soul of the day, Stax, Atlantic, Motown.

We started going to a coffee bar called the Bee-Gee, White Horse Street, just off Boar Lane. It was a smallish venue, with a jukebox and little seating booths, but also a bit of a dance area. They had incredible acts on there; Long John Baldry, Rod Stewart, and we took it over as 2nd generation mods, everyone used to do gear, or at least we did.

I wasn't allowed a scooter initially, but later I borrowed one, which caused a bit of a commotion, so my mum persuaded my dad to let me have one, to stop me doing it again. This would have been '68.

One of the lads I met in town had been going to the Wheel, and he took me over there in the summer of '68. He even very kindly sent me over to Bradford to buy gear beforehand, so we'd be all right. We started going most Saturdays, depending on who was playing; any Soul artists touring the UK at that time played there. I saw Edwin Starr, the Drifters, Junior Walker, and a cross-section of Soul artists.

Scotch Andy DJ'd on Friday nights at the Central, as did my mate Denis Billingham, and we were going down there at the same time as the Wheel, around '69/'70. It was always a good night out; what's not to like about somewhere that's underground and plays Soul with a decent dancefloor?

The week after the Wheel closed, in early '71, we went to a club in Wakefield, the Metro Bistro, downstairs on the Bull Ring, where one of the lads had persuaded the owner to put an all-nighter on. About a hundred people turned up for the first one, but the week after they were coming from all over because there was nowhere else to go, and it lasted for about six weeks. I worked there, on the door, behind the bar, all except the last night when it got busted. Flash, one of the DJs, asked me to put a record on while he went to the toilet, but unfortunately a big drop of condensation fell from the ceiling onto the arm and knocked it off the record. Not a great DJing debut. The night it got busted was Flash's 21st, and he'd invited a small crowd of us to go to Keighley with him to celebrate. When we got back to Leeds, we decided not to go to the Metro because we didn't have any gear, but Flash managed to get a lift off someone because he was DJing, and ended up getting arrested. It was headline news in the *Yorkshire Evening Post*.

A bit later, Denis and I set up a night at Hernando's, Hennies, in Harehills. Joan wasn't right happy with Denis, because he was a Central DJ and this was competition, so she sacked him. It hadn't been run as a club for some years, but we persuaded the owner to give it a go. You went in on the ground floor, up some stairs to a seating area, with a nice espresso coffee machine, which we had Pete Dillon working on, then up a 2nd flight of stairs to the dancehall with a DJ booth. All of a sudden, we had hundreds coming in, but we were only running for about four weeks when we got busted. Someone shouted, "Squad's here," and all of a sudden, there were drugs scattered all over the floor. They searched everyone and put a sticker on you once you'd been processed, with your hands on your head. Me and Dennis were allowed to walk around, as we were in charge, so we put The Reflections on the deck, except we were singing "just like Duromine & Durafet". Only two people ended up getting arrested, one silly sod who had his gear in a prescription bottle that he'd thrown on the floor, with his name on it!

The Central really came into its own at that time, there was nowhere else to go, and it was right there, on home turf. I can't remember many of the tunes from those days, because I was far more interested in socialising and dropping gear, but I've got one or two I bought back then that stick in my mind; Chris Jackson – 'I'll Never Forget You', Chubby Checker – 'At The Discotheque', Platters – 'Washed a Shore', not the ultra-rare tunes that have become a more recent phenomena.

One infamous night we were on a coach going to a nighter in Huddersfield when it got pulled over by the police near the football ground, and I quickly hid my stash down the side of the seat. When the police got on, they searched you, noted your seat number, and then put a sticker on you to show you'd been processed. When they got to my seat, they lifted the cushion, shone the torch underneath, but my gear, which had been trapped down the side, flew in a perfect arc and landed straight down the back of the seat, my wife Judy and I with our hearts in our mouths, and was never found. We all got strip searched, but another lucky escape.

The nighters started at the Central at the beginning of '73, but I'd got married in '72, so wasn't going as much. I was going up to that point, and helped Willy on the door, not that he needed any help. It was brilliant; I got paid to have a chat, drop gear and dance. I drifted along in this wonderful bubble, the atmosphere, the quality of the tunes, the socialising. It meant a lot to me, it was a Leeds based gig, it was ours and put Leeds on the map as a Soul city. We all have a common bond of Soul music and amphetamines.

Richard Minott's story:

I started going into town, and pretty soon Lulu's café. I'd go down there after school and on Saturday afternoons, usually with the lads I was playing football with. In those days there weren't many black people going into town at all, most stayed around Chapeltown. Initially I was just shopping for clothes and records, but then got attracted to the action at Lulu's. I often went with Calvin Wilkes, who was one of the first black professional players for Leeds RL. Lulu's had a reputation for being a bit rough, but I never found it that way. There weren't many places that were playing black music that you could safely go to, but at Lulu's you met up with likeminded people, drawn in by the music, it was a very multicultural crowd. I went for the music and socialising, it didn't matter who you were, where you came from or what you looked like. This has always drawn me to places I went to and the friends I have made over the years. It was all about feeling comfortable rather than having to dress or behave a certain way. There were people who dressed mod down there, but it was more inclusive than that.

I'd always grown up in a multicultural environment. Although I lived in between Scott Hall and Chapeltown, I went to St John Bosco's, where there was only one other black guy. All of my friends from those early years were white, but race was not something I consciously thought about until much later. When I went into town, colour didn't matter to me, there were people I liked and those I didn't, determined by their attitude.

Big Adrian was the mod icon at Lulu's, he was the one everyone followed. It was a typical 60s café bar, with plastic sheets on the tables, and the food, coffee and prices were all reasonable. There was always music there, particularly downstairs, and it was a style of music I liked, not the charts, more soulful stuff. You could have a little dance, but it is not somewhere you would want to dance all night, it wasn't very big.

I can't remember if Lulu's closed, but somehow we gravitated towards the Central on various nights, Friday nights and Saturday afternoons. It was a much bigger venue, and that's where the crowd moved to. I went down with Donald Caesar, Calvin Wilkes and Sonny Small. The music was all Soul, Motown and Stax. This would have been '69-'70.

The old Mecca was another venue we'd go to, where Hunter DJ'd. There was some trouble one night, with a racial overtone, and they were all waiting for us outside. I looked around for something to defend myself. All I could find was a metal toilet roll holder. Outside there was a bit of a standoff, and I brandished it, and as a result got banned from the club! The only man to be found guilty of being in possession of an offensive toilet roll holder.

From that point, it was exclusively the Central for me, as its policies were so different to all the other clubs in Leeds. The people there were not big drinkers, and hence there was very little trouble, no one getting pissed, fighting and being obnoxious, which was the norm elsewhere. People came for the music, to dance and have a good time. I remember Willie Richardson being on the door, who thought he was the bee's knees (and few would argue with that). There was also his brother Tony, but I knew their younger brother Walter. To be honest, there was always an atmosphere with them there; It didn't take much to piss them off. I never fell foul of them, but a lot of people did.

I was straddling two worlds at the time, down at the Central, and then after it closed back home to Chapeltown when we'd often go on to a Blues. They were a bit grubby and nasty, filled with smoke, but they played good music and were free. The famous ones were Kusa-Pek, Sonny's and Darkies. There was some dodgy stuff going on in some of these places, but if you only dipped in and out, you didn't get involved. There were one-offs, people would just do one to sell their wares and pay a bill.

We started going to Primo when some of the crowd moved on down there. I knew Oky from around town, there was a connection between Calvin's girlfriend and a shop Oky was assistant manager in. In those days in some of the shops, you could go and have a coffee and a chat in the backroom when you were shopping in town. That's how Oky and I became friends and how I ended up back at the Central again for the Jazz Funk night. That's how I got to know you; Oky was the common denominator.

It was all about going out, hearing good music, having a dance and meeting up with friends. The Central was one of those places where you always got that, where I could enjoy myself without any aggravation.

Steve Luigi's story:

The reason the Central has a distinct smell is that it was a waxworks. People think it's damp, but it's not, it's the wax and they'll never get rid of it, it's in the walls.

I started going in '69 after the Spinning Disc. I heard about the Central from the mods and scooter boys. All the Lulu's boys used to go there, and I knocked around with them, they were some of the hardest lads in Leeds and I saw some violent stuff. I bought my first scooter off one of the Lulu's, John Sweeney, who showed me how to ride it. I went to the same school as John, St. Josephs in Hunslet, so we were already good mates. Not many of Lulu's were into Soul, only a small number of them.

I was in Jumbo buying my weekly fix of Tamla Motown, and a lad called Dave Maltas came up to me and asked me if I liked Northern Soul, which was the first time I'd heard the term. I said I didn't really know what it was, but he said, "Tonight if you fancy it, if you can get yourself to the Queens hotel, there's a coach going the Torch in Stoke-on-Trent." I went, and there was no looking back, which would have been '71. Dave Maltas, who has a better memory than me, said we would have gone to the Central before the Torch, but not everyone who went was into Soul music, it was a bit of mod stuff, a bit of ska, Tamla, a bit of everything. That's the reason he asked me if I was into Northern Soul, because not everyone who went to the early Central was. It didn't turn into a 100% Northern Soul club until '71.

That night at the Torch changed my life, and I met some of my best and longest friends there, including Dave Maltas and Chris Mallows, both of whom still go to the Central all-dayers, Chris being one of the original Central DJs. Tony Banks had been DJing there long before I started going. Lads who'd gone to the Twisted Wheel started bringing their own records and getting the DJs to play them, which is how the Northern stuff started coming into it. Tony Jackson and Keith Atkinson asked Len Cave if they could do a Northern night, and he agreed to give it a try for a couple of weeks to see how it went. The rest is history.

I knew Tony Banks reasonably well because I'd talk to him about records, and he'd show me what he was playing and the labels they were on. He was a radio DJ, and he got all the promotional copies sent to him, all the Stateside demos, Tamla Motown and Columbia demos.

The name Northern Soul wasn't used then, but he had one of the best Northern collections in the country without really knowing it; we referred to it as Uptown Soul. I remember when he brought out the record Jimmy Thomas – 'Beautiful Night', on his TB Supersoul label, and we took a load down to the Torch and I sold them for 50p each, for every one I sold, I got 25p. There were rumours he knew Simon Soussan, who was knocking around Leeds at the time, but I can't remember him actually going to the Central.

It's our worst nightmare that we snuff it, and our collections end up in a clearance sale, as sadly happened to Tony Banks. Since I've started collecting again, I've got them all catalogued, the artist, the title, the label, and importantly, the current value. I've said to my wife, when I go, there's the records, there's the list, make sure you get what they are worth for them. My mate Paul Emmonds knows the records I have and what they are worth, and if I go first, he will help my wife sell them.

I got into House music and out of Northern because it had got too commercial, just after they took the cameras in to Wigan Casino for the documentary *This England*, and I sold all my Northern records to buy House records. I've regretted it ever since. I know the guy I sold them to, Brian the Barber, and I keep asking if I can come and look at them, just to remember what I had. He won't let me because he says I'll want them back, the miserable sod, LOL. Since then, though, I have amassed far more records than I had back then and think I have got most of the ones back that I sold.

The people I remember from the early Central are the people I still know to this day; Dave Maltas, Pete Dillon, Chris Mallows, Keith Atkinson, Twink. I got to know the DJs because I was well into the music. The atmosphere at the Central was second to none, it's buried in the walls, and when you play Northern Soul, it comes out again. It's like someone bottled it, and they release it when we do the all-dayers, it's still there. When I first went down to start the all-dayers again, I cried, I'd not been down there for 30 odd years.

I got into DJing because I had a lot of records and Len Cave liked me. I went down one week, and I spoke to Len, and said I'd got loads of records, but that I was only playing them to myself, and wanted to play them to other people; any chance of doing a spot? He said to bring a box down the following week and to do a bit. Because I was a dancer, I knew what people wanted to dance to, so I just played a full set of out and out dancers. The floor was packed for the whole session, and when I came off, Len came up to me and asked if I wanted to be resident, that's how it happened to me, and some 50 years later, DJing is still my profession.

I was bang into the new stuff also, and was going to Blackpool Mecca and Cleethorpes, and loved dancing to it. I came second in the Cleethorpes pier competition, and everyone said I should have won. I also came second at Wigan Casino, but the lad who won was a better dancer. I can't remember what year it was, but I do remember a lad called Ackers, who wore a flat cap and was at the front of the stage, and when I was dancing and trying to concentrate, I kept looking down and his hat was flapping from side to side and I couldn't stop laughing but came second anyway.

There are so many records it's hard to remember, but one of my all-time favourites was Mike Post – 'Afternoon Of The Rhino', the reason being I was really good at spinning, and when I was dancing and it came to the end part, and it stops and goes "err err" I'd stop spinning and do a knee drop, I loved that bit. Another of my other favourites is The Younghearts – 'A Little Togetherness', because it's just a wall of sound, you couldn't fit anything else in there, it's just amazing, the lyrics are brilliant. The one that makes me cry is Tobi Legend – 'Time Will Pass You By'. How many times have we heard that record, but every time it gives me tingles and tears, the words are just so true, listen to them and you'll see what I mean.

Moses Smith, Jimmy Soul Clark, there are just so many great records, Solomon King – 'This Beautiful Day'. There was a guy sitting in the seating area at the Central, behind the DJ stand, and he was selling a copy of Solomon King for £30, but I couldn't afford it; £30 was three weeks wages in those days, but I've had copies since then. Where did records like 'Afternoon of the Rhino' come from? How did someone go into a studio and record something like that? There was no such term as Northern Soul back then, and it wasn't done as a theme tune for anything, so why? With a full orchestra in a recording studio, it would have blown my mind to have been there.

In terms of artists, I've always been a big fan of Gladys Knight, I've seen her a few times, in fact I got into her dressing room, officially by the way, I didn't sneak in, I'm not a stalker. We saw her in Sheffield theatre club. There was me, Pete Dillon, Chris Mallows and Dave Maltas, and after the show, we asked the doorman if there was any chance of seeing Gladys. He asked and she said yes. We were stood in the dressing room with all the Pips, I got a kiss, and her and her brother 'Bubba' signed my Central card, which I've still got. Absolute madness. Can you imagine trying to do that today, they'd call the police. I also saw Al Green in Birmingham, but it's hard to single artists out, there were so many. Jackie Wilson, every track a stormer, and he died penniless and got ripped off by record companies, all that shuffling on one leg; it's easy to see where Michael Jackson got his ideas from.

You can't really define Northern Soul; it covers so many styles. There were white artists singing in the style of black artists (like Jerry Fuller, Paul Anka), and black artists singing in the style of white artists, trying to sell records. A lot of Northern Soul was made in the hope it would be heard and picked up by Berry Gordy, and they'd get signed to Motown. I spoke to Eugene Thomas, the lead singer with The Epitome of Sound, and I asked him what kind of music did you think you were recording when he recorded 'You Don't Love Me', because obviously there was no such thing as Northern Soul at the time? He said we just saw it as R&B. He'd contacted me because would you believe it, he'd heard my radio show and asked me if I'd play a new record he'd made. I said of course, and that's when we got chatting. True to his word, he sent me a signed demo and I played it. Unfortunately, Eugene passed away recently, leaving one of the biggest Northern Soul anthems behind for us to enjoy forever.

I got back into Northern Soul after a 15-year break. I was on the computer one day and was looking for something that had nothing to do with Northern (no, not that, something to do with House music) and this thread came up out of the blue, Night Owl, and I of course recognised it as a Northern Soul record by Bobby Paris. I clicked on the link and 'Open The Door To Your Heart' by Darrell Banks started playing, and I burst into tears. There were tears running down my face, I was buzzing and tingling, and I thought I need to get back into it, this is where my heart is.

I went on Soul Source one day, and Pete Dillon asked if anyone had any old photos of Leeds Central. I said, "Hi Pete, not seen you for years," and so I uploaded some photos. I got to thinking the Central was still in people's hearts, people still remembered it and loved it, so I asked on Soul Source when is someone going to do a reunion? After a week and no reply, so I put underneath, "Fuck it then, I'll do it." I pulled together all the old memorabilia I had, and I rang up HiFi Club, which had been the Central venue. They knew me because of the House stuff, and I asked if we could have a meeting about doing something. They invited me down, John the manager and the club manageress met me, and I asked them if they knew any of the history of the venue, but all they knew was it had been a rocker club and mod club. I then told them it had been one of the biggest Northern Soul clubs in the country and showed them all the old write ups and photos, and they nearly fell off their chairs. I asked what they thought about starting it up again and they replied, "When?" I said it would have to be a Saturday night, but they couldn't, that night was packed with students and a busy one for the club, but they said, "How about Friday night?" I said no, people would have to travel and some worked Saturdays, so we compromised on Sunday all-dayers. That's how it started, almost 10 years ago now.

I'm nearly in tears here, you don't know how proud this has made me, the little fella who used to go down there dancing; people took the piss out of me in the early days. I got bullied a lot in my younger days, people would call me all sorts because I was small and had eczema at the time, but I am so proud of myself, to be the one that has brought it back to being one of the best clubs in the country, loved and attended by thousands from all over; people come up to me in the club and thank me for starting it up again. I was one of the young outsiders, compared to all the big guys who'd been into it for years, but to be the one who had the balls to go and set it up again, and do it properly in the original venue, with the original DJs and the original music, makes me so proud.

Steve Caesar's story:

Well, my memories of Leeds Central are very happy ones. Let me give you a bit of background.

I arrived in England shortly after my 13th birthday, in December '69, firstly in London, and then my brother and I were transferred to Leeds, where our parents and my two elder brothers resided. My elder brother and I were sent to Coldcotes school, quite a distance away, and were the only black boys there. I gravitated towards the cool crowd, who had what you could describe as a mod sensibility.

I was first introduced to the Central in Jumbo records, on the balcony in the beautiful Art Nouveau Queens Arcade, where I met Steve Luigi, Chris Mallows and other Soul fans. We were all avid readers of *Blues & Soul*, and eagerly tried to track down the records we'd read about.

I also went to the Spinning Disk on Sunday mornings, when I was still at school and about 15, which was in the County Arcade and played Soul, Motown and pop, the Miracles, Supremes, Stevie Wonder and that kind of thing. That's where my love of danceable Soul music began.

I then started going to the old Mecca on a Monday and Tuesday; Monday was for the older crowd, the over 18s, and Tuesday was under 18s. Hunter Smith DJ'd on Monday nights. I'm guessing I went with my older brother Donald, Richard Minnot and Calvin Wilkes, but often I'd go on my own. They'd play stuff like Archie Bell – 'Here I Go Again' and Formations – 'Top Of The Stairs', Tams, Tami Lynn and Motown. I have always been independent and didn't really knock around with a gang, there was no one around where I lived really into it like me. These were the records that got me into the more upbeat Soul.

I was an apprentice at Yorkshire Switch Gear, and I'd go to day-release at EITB. There was a guy from Pontefract called Paul Vors, and he was into the music and introduced me to the Gospel Classics – 'More Love', and talked about the Central. It was all word of mouth. I had also met these guys from Bradford at the Mecca, and they too told me about the Central, and so I just started going down on my own on Friday nights and immediately fitted in. I'd catch the number 20 bus to the Headrow and just go straight down, as I wasn't really going into pubs at this time, this would have been about '71. I was new to the scene, so I didn't really pay attention to the DJs, but I'd seen Tony Banks's name on the flyers. I was learning, I didn't really know about the Twisted Wheel or the Torch back then.

The Central crowd were the real deal, they were already seasoned clubbers and welcomed me in with open arms, I found the right place as a young lad settling into life in the UK. Hearing records like 'Please Let Me In', 'Ain't No Soul', 'Back Street', just made want to hear more of this great music. The DJs were Tony Banks (TB Super Soul was his moniker) and Twink, and then others who played were Chris Mallows, Steve Luigi, and later on Ian Dewhirst would feature and become the principal DJ. People I remember in the early days seemed to be from the surrounding areas, people from Selby (Paul Temple), York, Bradford, Harrogate (Andy Wilson), Hull, Barnsley, Castleford.

My first impressions of the Central was that it was small, dark and intimate; I'd never been to a club before the Mecca, so this was all still relatively new to me. My only other experience of music and dancing at that point had been house parties in Chapeltown with friends and family, and memories of carnival in St Kitts.

I was still new in the country and finding my way, but I never felt confined to my part of town, Chapeltown, and was keen to explore, driven by curiosity and a sense of new-found freedom. I grew up with my aunt, and she stayed in St Kitts, but she had a strong expectation for me that I would succeed in my new country. I had no fear or any negativity holding me back.

I was always a confident dancer, always had rhythm. We grew up dancing in St Kitts, at carnival and at parties, dancing in the streets, it was natural. I started dancing in England at the Spinning Disc and Mecca but adapted my style by copying others down at the Central.

Archie Bell – 'Here I Go Again' was always an early favourite. I knew Archie Bell from the Caribbean because 'Tighten Up' had been a big international record. Otis, Sam and Dave, Percy Sledge had all been massive artists in the West Indies. That Stax sound was familiar to me. The music was joyous and uplifting and made you want to dance; that beat and funkiness just made you want to move your feet.

The Central all-nighters started in '73 after the Torch had closed. I remember everyone talking about the Torch, and in particular the night Major Lance performed down there. I wouldn't have been allowed to go, I'd never been out of Leeds at the time, so going to Stoke would have been like going to France. I did later see him at the Castleford Civic Centre, and he was amazing.

The first Central all-nighter came, but I'd never stayed out all night, and that was a different kettle of fish. I remember getting dressed in my bedroom and trying to pluck up courage to ask my parents, but in the end I didn't. When the second one came around, I plucked up courage and asked, and surprisingly was allowed to go. Richard Searling DJ'd at this one. The crowd were milling around outside, dressed immaculately in blazers, some with Torch badges on them, and others with single black gloves, like we'd seen worn by the US athletes on the podium at the Mexico Olympics. Richard came up from the main road, record box in hand, and the crowd parted to let him through, like Moses parting the waves.

The tunes Richard played were new to me. Linda Jones – 'Just Can't Live My Life', Shawn Robinson – 'My Dear Heart', Jerry & Paul – 'The Catwalk', Rose Batiste – 'Hit And Run', Alice Clark –'You Hit Me', Elsie Strong – 'Just Ask Me', all the tunes that had been big at the Torch and VaVa's. The night was amazing, hot, sweaty and absolutely packed. I floated up those steps at the end of the night, it was a transformative experience.

The Central all-nighters were once a month, and I think started in February '73 and ran until November or December. I didn't go to the infamous all-nighter that was raided, as Christmas was coming up and money was tight. I attended all but the first one in those months; that is until the talk of this new all-nighter that was happening in a town called Wigan. I knew I had to be there, and in the November of '73 I attended my first Wigan all-nighter. I was (and still am) a Leeds United fan, and we were playing Burnley away. I travelled there complete with holdall and intended to travel to Wigan from Burnley after the game by Wallace Arnold coach. Things didn't go to plan, but I bumped into Andy Wilson who knew me from the Central, and he invited me to come with them, as he too was going to Wigan that night. So back I went to Leeds with them, past my home, to Harrogate where Andy lived above a pub with his mum and dad, and then all the way back to Wigan. Wigan was an eye opener; my first major all-nighter and I took to it like a duck to water, the music, the people, just mind-blowing, a musical sensation.

Petrol was syphoned to fill up the car, and then we were on the way to Wigan. A collection of "green and clears" were divvied up, which I had never seen and certainly not taken before. I was this young naïve black guy, but allegedly took a couple and I had the time of my life; full of energy and a feeling of euphoria, alert and not out of it, but combined with the atmosphere and the music it was electric and off the scale. You had all the ex-Torch goers, people from all over the country.

And what was even more unbelievable was that the following year I was the winner of the first Wigan anniversary dance competition, a great achievement having only been in England for such a short time and to have become part of such an important movement. I don't know what made me enter it, I'm guessing somebody egged me on, maybe my friend from Leeds, Steve Walwyn, but It's thanks to honing my dancing skills at the Central that first set me on the path.

I still went to the Central on Friday nights, but Wigan had become the centre of my universe in '74. Also, I'd been to Blackpool Mecca twice, once with the guys from Bradford and once with the guys from work, although they didn't go to the Mecca. After we'd finished our training at college, the lads I worked with were organising a celebratory coach trip, and I suggested Blackpool, albeit with ulterior motives. Off we went; they went on the beer and I went to the Mecca, but I did go to the pub and pleasure beach with them all first. An Asian lad called Muntas came with me. He wasn't really into Soul but didn't drink and so was looking for a way to escape the group. The Highland room was like entering another world. The people were so cool, the music was incredible, stuff I'd never heard before.

My early Central memories include:

- J.J. Barnes – Please Let Me In.
- Jerry Williams – If You Ask Me.
- The Showmen – Our Love Will Grow.

- Donald Height – Talk Of The Grapevine.
- Joan Moody – We Must Be Doing Something Right.
- Invitations – What's Wrong With Me Baby.
- O'Jays – I Dig Your Act.
- Denise Laselle – A Love Reputation.
- Jimmy Conwell – That Beating Rhythm.
- Alexander Patton – A LI'll Loving Sometime.
- Frank Polk – Love Is Dangerous.
- Jerry Cook – I Hurt On The Other Side.
- Archie Bell – Here I Go Again.
- First choice – This Is The House.
- Darrell Banks – Open The Door To Your Heart.
- Rose Batise – Hit And Run.
- Detroit Emeralds – Feel The Need.
- The Fidel's – Try A Little Harder.
- The Shakers – One Wonderful Moment.
- Linda Jones – Just Can't Live My Life.

The Central meant a lot to me: acceptance in Britain, finding my place, just fitting in and enjoying life. It was a great release from the drudgery of work and brought a feeling of assimilation and integration, a place of safety, and a feeling of belonging and being amongst friends, many of whom have stayed with me my whole life.

Simon Andrews's story.

It's the early seventies, and I've graduated from listening to Soul and Reggae and Ska at all the local youth clubs, and now I'm hanging out with the cool kids at the Mecca in the centre of Leeds on Monday nights. The DJ is Hunter, and he plays an astonishing range of fantastic Soul music, everything from James Brown to Isaac Hayes – 'Shaft', Bob and Marcia – 'Young Gifted And Black' and Al Green.

But amongst these, he also plays some faster records, such as Robert Knight – 'Love On A Mountain Top', Archie Bell – 'Here I go Again', Isley Brothers – 'Tell Me It's Just A Rumour', and more.

I'm reading *Blues & Soul* every other week, scrutinising the Northern Soul column but didn't really get it at this point.

In the summer of '72 we had our first holiday without parents. My mate and our two girlfriends went to Newquay for a week in a caravan. We see there is a club called Coral a Go-Go, and outside it says it's a Soul club. There is James Brown, Four Tops and more written on posters, and so excitedly we go there one night. We walk in and we don't recognise one record, but the sounds were amazing! With hindsight, it was all Torch and Wheel Northern Soul. Things like Lenis Guess – 'Just Ask Me', Bobby Paris – 'Personally', Fuller Brothers – 'Time's A Wasting'. We were told this was Northern Soul, and we were instantly converted.

Back in Leeds we listened out for Hunter playing Northern. Then through *Blues & Soul* we realised there was a local Northern club, the Central.

So, one Friday we made the pilgrimage down those famous stairs. I could almost taste the atmosphere, the music was great, the people friendly. The only slightly odd thing was that we were dressed in the latest fashions, always cool (or so we thought) but we looked slightly out of place at the Central. Everybody else was wearing blazers and bags, the girls had white socks and big skirts, there's even a couple of berets. We loved it.

We were told the next one was an all-nighter. So, a quick chat with the parents, telling them it's open all night, but that we're going to come home just a little bit later than normal, and we get permission. We go for a drink first, and then down to the Central.

Again, the atmosphere is magical, but around one o'clock, things changed. Suddenly there is shouting, the music stops, the lights come on and it's full of police. I hear this amazing tinkling sound as everyone emptied their pockets, and all their pills rained onto the floor.

Police go around the club, pull out a bunch of people, some of whom I think they recognise, and take them off. About 50 are taken out, and the place empties of police. Everyone is standing around, a bit shocked. But then the police come back. It turns out they have an extra van and want more people to arrest, and I'm picked on and taken out, sitting in the back of a police van for the first and hopefully the last time.

We drive across Leeds and arrive at a big police garage in Woodhouse. I recognise it as the place where my dad works, who is a police inspector. There's probably about 50 or 60 of us, and about 20 to 30 policemen. We all queue up, first to give your urine samples, and I rib the policeman about rinsing the bottles out, about what a great career he has, perhaps not the wisest thing to do under the circumstances.

More standing around. It's now about two in the morning, and I'm a bit bored with all this, so I say to one of the policemen, "Do you know inspector Andrews?" "Yes," he says. "Well, he's my dad. He'll vouch for me; can I go home?" "Fuck off, shut up and get back in line," is the reply.

So more waiting. Eventually I'm sat down in front of the top plain-clothes police inspector, and he says that he'd heard I was Stan Andrews's lad. He says they are taking my test anyway, and that I'd hear from them in due course. "If the test is clear, you're okay. If it's not, well..."

With that, I was told I could go, strolling back across Leeds with a couple of other lads who clearly knew the scene much better than I did. They told me that raids like this were pretty normal at nighters, and I learnt a lot about the scene on that walk back to town. The Central was still going, so I picked up my girlfriend and headed home.

In the morning I was asked why we got home so late, so I told the story. As you can imagine, that didn't go down well, my dad just didn't speak to me for weeks. My mum said if I'd done anything to damage my dad's career that would be the end of it, or words to that effect.

After that, my dad didn't say much, but did read out loud everything in the papers about drugs and the Northern Soul scene, always prefaced by, "Your mates are in the papers again." Then one day, my dad tells me he's had a phone call from the drug squad and that I'm all clear. After that, things got a bit more back to normal.

A few months later, I asked my dad if he knew an inspector "Blogs". He said yes and so do you; he's the one who was in charge of the drug squad the night you got arrested. "Why do you ask?" said my dad. "Well, he came into the bank today (where I worked) wanting a loan to buy a car. I turned him down and he wasn't very happy." And now I realise why.

Rick Cooper's story:

I remember Leeds Central very well, as it was one of the best clubs I went to in my younger days. I went to Leeds in 1971, supposedly to study at the polytechnic. Student social life was based around pubs, with the occasional long-haired group live at the Student Union. Not my scene, and so I had to try to find something better.

The first thing was to locate a decent record shop, which I found was Jumbo Records. Initially this was at the back of a TV shop in the Merrion Centre, then moved to the first floor of one of the indoor arcades. Simon Soussan was quite often at Jumbo, although I don't think he ever bought anything. After a few months, I got to know some of the local lads, who bought their records there or just used it as a meeting place. I must have heard about the Central around this time and probably first went in late 1971. I don't remember who the DJs were, but I think at first the records played were mainly pressings and oldies. Some of the people who went would take rare records for the DJ to play. The club's owners encouraged this, as they saw that more people were attending, some from places like Selby, York and Barnsley. Tony Banks was the main DJ and was a professional who had a large collection of UK releases; however, at this point I don't think he had the newer imports that were getting played. He went to the US in '72 or '73, and bought back some great stuff, as well as "finding" 1,000 copies of Jimmy Thomas – 'Beautiful Night' on the TB label. I helped out on the DJing roster, as I was getting some good records from Simon Soussan and Martin Koppel, who had both left Leeds by then. Simon, before he started bootlegging, was finding loads of top records in good quantities. Martin, from his base in Toronto, made buying trips to the Detroit area where he found lots of Thelma, D Town, Revilot, Giant, Golden World etc. Martin was a year above me at Leeds Poly, doing the same subject as I did, but I never knew him then, which was a lost opportunity. Bostock's stall at Bradford market also had masses of great records, so it was fairly easy to build a decent collection.

As the Friday sessions were very popular, someone suggested trying a Saturday all-nighter. This would have been around '73. These went very well, even though the Torch nighters were running at that point. I think there was probably three or four nighters, when one night it was rudely interrupted by the West Yorkshire DS. This put an end to the all-nighters and may have stopped the Friday night sessions for a while. I'd returned back over the Pennines late '73, so only went to the later sessions a couple of times in '74 –'75.

Jean Smith's story.

I had been going to night clubs from the tender age of 16 before I went to the Central, such as the Starlight Club in Huddersfield, and the Mecca in Wakefield. I knew that I loved the music I was listening to, but as yet had not named it Northern Soul. The DJs at the Mecca, Frankie Johnson and Paul Rowan, played brilliant sounds and are still doing so to this day. Having made friends there, I heard good things about the Central, and so one weekend in early 1973, my best friend Denise and I got the train from Huddersfield to Leeds for our first of many trips there. The Central experience outshone anything that had gone before, the music, the dancing, the Soul community, and the atmosphere; we were feeling 'Ten Miles High', it was what 'living for the weekend' was all about.

We became part of a crowd, where the fashions were just right, inexpensive and understated but smart dance wear. Some dancers excelled, while others like myself felt the music and became part of the whole on the dancefloor. One of my boyfriends at this time was a bit of a 'bad lad', but he was a great dancer, plus he had a super record collection; I've heard he turned out well in the end. You could buy records at the club, and I bought one or two, but mainly I recorded them on my portable cassette recorder, which I would place on a shelf and leave running until the tape ran out. On Sundays, my friend and I would play it back, learning the tracks and trying to chill before work on Mondays. I feel nostalgic now whenever I hear 'The Girl Across The Street' by Moses Smith, because my soulmate Denise lived across the street from me, and I am still so sad that she died from cancer in her early forties. One of my favourite records that reminds me of great Central times is 'If You Ask Me' by Jerry Williams. When I got my *Blues & Soul* magazine, I'd check out what was being played in all the clubs, and it was not long before we were travelling across the country to other venues every weekend, Friday to Sunday. Quite often you would see me in my favourite top, sporting the two badges of the Central and Wigan Casino, both close to my heart, but the Central was my first.

I met many lifelong friends on the Soul scene, including my husband, Kenny, in 1974. Along with our fabulous friends from Huddersfield, Pauline and Charlie Atkinson, Dave and Ann Clegg, Scoff and Karen, we had the time of our lives. Alas, three of these soulies are no longer here to continue the journey, so we four feel truly blessed. When we had our son in 1979, the scene as we knew it had passed its best, and Kenny and I settled down to family life. Having dropped out and lost touch with everyone, it wasn't until

2012, when the kids had grown up and the records were in the loft, that we happened to go to a Northern Soul do at our local WMC. We had never stopped loving the music, and here was a room full of people reliving the dream. Being a 'chatty lass', I soon got talking to Mike Eastwood and Marlene Salter, who told me that the Central had re-opened, and was being run by our old friend, Steve Luigi. They said, "Are you on Facebook?" to which I replied, "No, I don't bother with that." They said, "Well, you want to, because nearly all you old mates are on there." And they were! Before we knew it, we were on our way to the next Leeds Central Soul Club all-dayer. I wondered if it would be a disappointment, but no, I could only say wow! As I went down those famous stairs, and that wonderful sound came up, the part of me inside that was going back to the original years jumped with joy. We were reunited with so many previous regulars; some instantly recognisable, some less so. The bond we had shared all those years ago came flooding back, we had all danced and clapped to the same beat and felt the same chill down our spines when hearing the intros to the classic tracks.

Now in 2020, the dates for the upcoming all-dayers are already in my calendar. DJ Twink journeys up to stay with us the night before, and we are playing sounds from his box until the early hours. I have my own little collection, small but beautiful, each one evoking precious memories. After a bacon butty breakfast, we catch the 110 'soul bus' from Wakefield to Leeds, along with Marlene, Mike and Lynn, and then we meet up once more with Pauline and Charlie, Stephanie and Lesley, plus the 'Whitelock's drinking gang'. Once more we are part of a wonderful crowd, who delight in being together. Hugs all round, a few drinks, a squeeze of Luigi, then down the stairs to Soul heaven, dancing and appreciating Northern Soul at its best, top DJs and a great club.

Jeff Leighton's story:

I first went to the Central in 1975, when I was 19 years old. I was certainly a member by then, as I still have my membership card which was valid until 31-Aug-1976. I grew up in Leeds, although haven't lived there since 1982.

I remember in the early to mid-seventies buying Reggae records at Jumbo Records, tunes such as 'Skank in Bed' by Scotty and Lorna Bennett, 'Duppy Gunman' by Ernie Smith, and 'Dat' by Pluto Shervington. They used to have adverts in the shop for the International Soul Club, and I particularly remember an advert for an all-nighter at Queens Hall featuring Major Lance and JJ Barnes. Unfortunately, at that time those names didn't mean anything to me, I knew little about the Northern scene, and so didn't go. I also remember they had a flyer for a Soul club event in a frame hanging on the wall, which with hindsight I'm guessing was probably an advert for a big night at the Torch, possibly the last all-nighter held there. As well as buying records, I also bought *Blues & Soul* magazine, and that further sparked my interest in Northern Soul.

I'd go to a pub in Leeds city centre called the Precinct, which had a DJ who played pop Soul records, and a dancefloor which looked like a boxing ring. I think that was the first time I saw lads dancing on their own. Pop Soul was very popular in the charts and on the radio, with artists such as The Three Degrees, The Detroit Emeralds, George McCrae, The Hues Corporation, MFSB as well as all the Tamla Motown classics.

If I went to a 'do' around this time, the favourite records would be songs such as 'Sweet Soul Music' by Arthur Conley, 'Land of a Thousand Dances' by Wilson Pickett, and 'Ghost In My House' by R Dean Taylor. It was clear then that Soul tunes with a dance beat were popular, and I wanted to discover more.

Wigan Casino all-nighter had opened in September 1973, and I wanted to go to the first anniversary in September 1974, but couldn't get tickets, and so eventually ended up going there for the first time around October or November 1974. I went with my mates Al and Ackers, on the train from Leeds City station to Manchester, and then on to Wigan.

I first went to the Central around the same time, and for the next two or three years I became a regular, as well as making infrequent trips to other Soul venues in the region. I remember going to the Cat's Whiskers in Meanwood, Raquel's in Wakefield city centre, Samantha's in Sheffield city centre, the Cow & Calf Hotel at Ilkley, Yeadon Town Hall, and to the Buffs Club at Keighley.

I remember the Central as a Friday night out in town and it being a really popular place, open from 8pm to 1.00am. You have to remember that at that time the pubs closed at 10.30pm and going to a night club until 2.00am, such as the Mecca in the Merrion Centre, meant having to dress up to get in, and you could only listen to pop Soul and chart pop records, while the young women danced around their handbags, and the young men stood around the edge of the dancefloor watching. Also, you were supposed to be at least 21 years old.

The Central played proper Northern Soul, the blokes danced on their own, and there were as many men dancing as there were women. The DJ I remember most was Paul Rowan, who played stuff like 'Ever Again' by Bernie Williams, 'What Kind of Lady' by Dee Dee Sharp, and the instrumental 'Thumb A Ride' by the Earl Wright Orchestra. The DJ most people will know is Steve Luigi, but I'm sure there were others whose names I can't remember. Frank also DJ'd there, and I remember him playing more modern tracks, which were also popular at the Cleethorpes Pier all-nighter, such as 'Ton of Dynamite' by Frankie 'Love Man' Crocker, and 'Summer in the Parks' by The East Coast Connection.

I remember walking down the steps into the Central and getting a buzz from the atmosphere almost immediately. The club is oblong-shaped, and on descending the stairs you are entering at one corner, and so can see across the whole of the club. There would be lots of people you knew, and we all had our own type of greeting and special Soul handshake.

We'd occupy the same bit of the club each week, me and my mates at the middle of the right-hand side. We were all from North Leeds, suburbs such as West Park, Horsforth, Cookridge, and Tinshill. Next to us, in the back right-hand corner, was usually Steve from the Moortown area who rode a Vespa scooter. The group in the middle of the club were from East Leeds, and were thought of (by me, at least) as the top soulies there. There was a guy called Gary Fields who had long hair, when we had all had ours cut short, who wore a brown leather bomber jacket and he was a good dancer there, and another guy called Steve who wore an authentic American bowling shirt with an embroidered picture on the back. I remember going to the first Cleethorpes Pier all-nighter with those guys around February 1976. We all went on a minibus from Leeds city centre and collected some others at the Manifesto Soul Club at Knottingley on the way. I remember standing on the pier in the cold, on a wet, dark night, waiting for the nighter to start, but it was worth it, though, as it was one of the best nights I had. The big tunes there were 'So Is The Sun' by The World Column, 'Cut Your Motor Off' by Black Nasty, and 'Lend a Hand' by Bobby Hutton.

My mate Ian was probably the second-best dancer at the Central, or at least I thought so. He was slim, had black curly hair and wore glasses, and always wore a mod suit made by a tailors called Trews on the Headrow. A lot of us at the Central had our trousers made at Trews, and I had two suits made there. I can't ever recall going to Wigan with Ian, but I remember going with him to Blackpool Mecca and to Cleethorpes Winter Gardens, both times getting a lift from other people.

The group in the front right-hand corner were not known to me, but I remember them coming from nearby towns to the South-West of Leeds such as Birstall, Cleckheaton, and Mirfield.

At the far-left side of the club was the seating area and the bar, where the older soulies were. They were like the 'elder statesmen' of the Soul scene, and they knew all the records being played, but they rarely danced. There's pictures of them on the sites, but I never really knew them, all I remember is that they all seemed to have beards!

(*"Steve from I think Moortown area who rode a Vespa scooter" I'm guessing is yours truly, as I do know Jeff from way back. Prior to the Vespa, I had a Lambretta, but as I needed transport for work, I had to get something more reliable. Controversial, I know*).

Steve Cook's story:

This is dedicated to all the Soul people who fell down the stairs and into the wall at the bottom. Let's be honest, we've all done that at some time, a sort of rite of passage. This is also dedicated to Soul people that fell up the stairs leaving the club, which hurt even more, as I know from experience.

The stairs' trial by ordeal, or you could say taking a leap of keep the faith, is part of the LCSC uniqueness as you enter from street level through a single door. You hear the murmur of the music playing as you walk into the darkly lit first flight of stairs, then turn at a right angle down the even darker second set. You then hear the rumble of the music and the anticipation of opening the door, knowing you were about to enter a Soul music paradise. Once inside there was no escape: the people are dancing, smiling and laughing, and there was no avoiding the excitement and enthusiasm of the crowd as you squeezed through them on the way to the bar. You became part of the scene, the club, the atmosphere, and from that moment there was no resisting the blaring Soul music, as if in a sound booth, eager for the good time you were about to experience. I still shiver with excitement, 45 years on, as I approach the door. I fondly remember when I slightly opened the door to the dancefloor, only to have it quickly slammed shut on me by the people dancing, them saying, "Do you mind, I'm dancing," to which I replied, "No, I don't mind, enjoy the night." Good times, and dancers always take priority.

I was always into music, right from Reggae to Rock 'n' Roll, but when Steve Caesar lent me some Northern Soul tapes it was wow, exactly what I was looking for, I was hooked. I was an apprentice with Steve at Yorkshire Switch Gear, and we always got along.

I'd hear Motown at the youth club and felt it was a bit poppy, but what amazed me was one of the tracks on the tape was Martha Reeves – 'One Way Out', and it was more of an R&B sound. I realised there was another side to Motown, all the B-sides and the stuff they didn't release. The other track I remember from that tape was The Gospel Classics – 'More Love That's What We Need', which I later learnt was written in reaction to the assassination of Dr Martin Luther King Jr.

I was looking for music and went to the Leeds Mecca and Samantha's. I noticed Caesar was always so upbeat when he came back from a Northern night, so I thought I'd go and sample it for myself. I decided to take my then girlfriend Patricia to Wigan Casino on the train. I told Caesar of my experience, and boy it was an experience getting to Wigan on British Rail in those days, and I told him how brilliant it had been, but that it was so far away. It's then that he suggested going to Leeds Central, so I decided to take Patricia on a night out down there, I was a bit Steve naïve in those days.

I was nervous about getting in: you had to be 21 to get into most clubs in those days, and at clubs like Cinderella Rocka Fella, women would wear ball gowns! I was expecting loads of bouncers, but there were none, only a fella sat at a desk, and he let us in no problem.

You had no choice but to walk through a floor of dancers, so you were already on the dancefloor without even trying, and then squeeze past everyone to get to the bar. The atmosphere was electric, and I thought *this is the place for me.* I loved all the 100mph stuff, there was no escape from the music, proper Soul. We were 30' down, people walking above us oblivious to this underground scene. I was about 18 at the time, in '73. My mind was popping, my ears were ringing, this was it for me. I didn't dance the first few times; I was too self-conscious and there were so many great dancers. It was great just people-watching, seeing their passion.

I'd heard some other lads from Belle Isle were into Northern, old school friends, so I hooked up with them at the Omnibus and started going with them, lads like big Mally, whose head nearly touched the ceiling at the Central. Mally actually DJ'd at the Omni, in a fashion, playing records through the tannoy system. Jeff, Paul and Roger Jackson were in the building trade and had a van, so we'd jump in that and go to the Central and Wigan. I bumped into you and Dave down there, and Gary Fields, Sam, little Melv (sadly departed). Seeing Mally at 6'6" talking to Melv at under 5' was a sight to behold.

When the Friday Northern nights stopped, I was still going to Wigan on Saturday, but then Jazz Funk nights started at the Central and we started going down there. The dancers were incredible, guys like Doville. I remember Jill having a squeezy bottle full of whisky, which she'd let us have a squirt of. We'd somehow get home on the scooters. I nearly knocked Sally Anne over one night; she ran out in front of me, and I couldn't stop, she didn't know whether to stick or twist, but luckily, I swerved round her.

As long as people are happy and dancing, that's the scene I want to be in. I never got involved with people or record politics, I just try and live a simple life. There were too many tunes to recall from the Northern days, most of which are gathering dust in my boxes, and which I mainly got from Soul Bowl, but I do specifically remember a couple of Jazz-Funkers, Slave – 'Just A Touch' and Kool and the Gang – 'Ladies Night'; we all used to do a fantastic rocking side to side dance to it.

If they hadn't let me into the Central all those years ago, my life wouldn't have changed. It opened up a whole new world for me and broadened my horizons, great music, great people, and that's why I want to thank everyone. Even today, if you can't enjoy yourself down there, you can't enjoy anywhere. The only things that have changed is they've taken the door away, so now when you fall down the stairs, you're straight onto the dancefloor, making an even more spectacular entrance. In addition, the bar can now serve more than two at a time, the toilets are not like outside loos, and the alcove-type seating that surrounded the dancefloor has gone. All changes for the better I would suggest, without losing the atmosphere.

A fantastic club that has changed my life, everyone shoulder-to-shoulder, it's a wonder we managed to dance, and all this happening in a basement 30 feet below street level, like a good Soul and Jazz Funk club should be.

Dave Raby's story:

I got into Northern Soul at Allerton Grange and their youth club. There was a lad called Dave Waller, who was from Manchester originally and a big City fan. He was in my year at school and used to play and dance to it on a Thursday night down there. I liked the popular Soul and Motown of the day, but this was something else. I'd go to Heaven and Hell at the bottom of the Headrow on a Monday night, and went to the Queens Hall all-nighter, the one with the stone floor that wrecked our shoes. I was only about 15 at the time. Somehow, I found out about the Central.

I moved into lodgings in Wakefield when I got a job at Walton pit as an underground worker. I was supposed to work five days a week, but having to get up at 04:30 was hard, and I'd sleep in a lot, I rarely managed to get a full week in! Every Friday, I would go through to Leeds and stay at my grandparents' In Kirkstall. I literally lived for the weekends and would call you up from a nearby phone box to ask if you were going to the Central and Wigan, and I can't remember you ever saying no!

I'd visit the Virgin record shop just down from the Precinct pub, as did most of the Soul crowd, due to the fact they always seemed to have import 45s for sale. The two guys who worked there were friendly, I think they were Carl and Klike. I can remember Steve Richmond finding original copies of The World Column and Candi Staton there, which were massive tunes at Blackpool Mecca at the time, and he only paid about 80p each for them.

At the Central you'd go down those steep steps and pay Derek, who was always welcoming despite our young age. We'd stand in the far corner, near where the stage is now. The older crowd congregated in the seating area at the other end. I remember it being slightly intimidating at first; I didn't think they were too keen on us young newcomers, but over time we got to know people and made many good friends down there. People I remember were John Drysdale, Tony Richardson (a very big lad, popular for his prescription slimming tablets), Spud, Mick Durant from Wakefield, Sam Davison, Jack Horner, Blake, Mally and you, Jill and Cooky obviously.

Eric Smith was one of the best dancers, as was Steve Luigi before his accident at Wakefield Mecca. Apparently, he was dancing and mistimed a swallow dive, and damaged his knob, allegedly asking the doctor to give him something for the pain, but to leave the swelling. LOL. (I have talked to Steve about this, and although he confirmed the swallow dive incident was true, the real reason he had to stop dancing was an industrial accident where he damaged his knee but agreed that the knob story was funnier than the knee, and for the story to remain). He assures me it healed nicely. Steve was the link between the old crowd and us.

I remember a night when some drunks came down and made a beeline for us for some reason; I had the type of face people loved to punch! I ended up getting into a 'tussle' with them. There was no bouncer, people just used to walk in off the street to find out what was going on down there. Luckily, I was able to defend myself, as I had acquired some of the 'noble art' skills from St. Patrick's and the White Rose boxing clubs.

Early tunes for me were things like Ike & Tina Turner – 'Dust My Broom', Platters – 'Washed Ashore'; I think Swish used to play them. I remember the night the management tried to sack Swish for some reason, and there being a backlash, the crowd shouting for his reinstatement. Later, Frank played some great stuff, Anderson Brothers, Sisters Love. Alan Rhodes played some good tunes, Volumes – 'Just Can't Help Myself' and Herbert Hunter – 'I Was Born To Love You'. Paul Rowan played things like The 5 Jays – 'Hey, Hey Girl', and Pat Brady played some good new discoveries.

One particularly memorable night for me was when my girlfriend of the day, Debbie, got me a copy of the Del Larks – 'Job Opening' for my birthday. She bought it off Ginger Taylor for £50, and he brought it down to the Central for her. Sadly, I had to sell it for £50 a few years later, during the miner's strike, I was skint! I could probably have got £60 if I'd been a better negotiator, as the last traded copy went for over eight thousand pounds. You took a picture of it for me, and I've still got it, but sadly not the record. Selling my collection was not one of my better decisions, but I didn't have a lot of choice. I have built it back up since, but don't think I'll ever get them all back, there is a price beyond which even I won't go!

When it turned to Jazz Funk, I continued to go with you and Cooky. I had grown a beard and bought a sheepskin coat at the time, my football manager phase. They were great nights, except for one when we couldn't get a taxi and I was walking back to Cooky's in the pouring rain, and my sheepskin got absolutely soaked. It must have weighed at least two stone when I got back, I was on my knees, and it took two weeks to dry out.

Ian Muscroft's story:

One of the first things I remember from the Central is seeing Eric at the bottom of the stairs, dancing to 'Night Owl' by Bobby Paris. Eric was a magnificent dancer and seemed to float above the dance floor, absolutely fantastic. Sometime later, I remember his then girlfriend, I think she was called Debra, wearing a yellow leather trouser suit, and when we went outside, they were in the same colour yellow car. From that point, Eric was referred to as having a matching car and girlfriend.

I can also remember when Ian Dewhirst was still known as DJ Frank. He went back to his real name when he started DJing with Paul Schofield, playing more contemporary Funk records.

My favourite record was The Tomangoes – 'I Really Love You', and I still love it to this day.

The Central was also a good spot to get a lift to Sheffield Samantha's all-nighter, with John Vincent announcing "Here's the Skullsnaps with Hang Up Your Hang Ups" in the strangest possible way, more like "Ang Up... ... ... YerangUps".

I always thought that the Central was a very friendly place and a super way to spend a Friday night. Once they got to know you on the door, you could get in without having to show your membership card, which made you feel very welcome.

I also remember when Paul was playing alongside Ian, that we had a shorts party, as the Central did get very hot. That was in the '70s, before wearing shorts became the norm, and we all got some strange looks as we walked through town on our way to the club.

Because it was the Central School of Dance and trained people in ballroom dancing, it had a proper sprung dancefloor, which helped dancing considerably. It is nice of Jeff to consider me the second-best dancer in the Central, and I am honoured, when you think of all the great dancers in there, to be even in the discussion.

As Glen Campbell said the last time we met, "We were the dancers in the group."

I seem to recall that the DJ booth was set up in front of a small lounge area, separated by gold-painted railings, and the lounge was maroon and seemed to be something from an earlier time, the late 60s or early 70s.

My main overriding memory of the Central is that it was a lovely friendly place to go and remained that way throughout; there is magic in those four walls.

David Okonofua's story (aka Oky):

I remember they had a night called El Centrico (the Downtown or Central in Spanish) and I went with my sister Anita, who is sadly no longer with us; she was a regular and could have given a great story. She knew Bill Richardson, Mr Universe, which is how I got in for nothing, particularly as I was underage. Anita was beautiful, had a big afro and looked a bit like Diana Ross.

I went around with the Hyde Park lot, my home turf, and was listening to a lot of Soul, Motown and Stax. We used to go to Outlook in Doncaster and then heard about the Central and were encouraged to come down. This would have been about '75. Paul Rowan, Frank and Twink were DJing at the time.

I remember a guy with bleached hair and white trainers, who just stood there and didn't dance. We'd stand in the back-right corner, a group of girls and boys, including Caesar. We knew Eric and nicknamed him Bruce Lee based on his ethnicity. He was a bit older and had gone to the Torch. He called himself Eric Smith for some reason, not his proper name of Saynor. Eric was a great dancer, the best down there. He'd have his long leather coat on and just glide about the floor. Caesar was also a great mover, he didn't go mad but just flowed with the rhythm, and Ian Muscroft was another good dancer.

There was a night just before Christmas, and Eric got into some bother with some skinheads, about six of them, that shouldn't have been there and had gone in to cause trouble. All Eric's old mates, who we thought were a bit handy, just stood there and let them batter him, scared to get involved, so I jumped in and pulled him out and sat him on the stage. I then picked up a chair to explain to the skinheads that beating up my mate was not the done thing, but as I swung it back, somebody grabbed hold of it and said, "Nice that you're helping out, but you don't need to do that." I didn't know him before, but that turned out to be Fred Ward, a nice but hard man. Lucky he stopped me, because just then the police came in. Me and Fred got on great after that.

I remember Mistura feat. Lloyd Michels – 'The Flasher' was big, and everyone getting really annoyed because it had been on *Top of the Pops* with some shit dancers. Stanley Woodruff – 'What Took You So Long' was another favourite. I always liked the newer style tunes, things like Mel Britt – 'She'll Come Running Back', Larry Saunders – 'On The Real Side', Case of Time – 'Manifesto' ("shop at Tesco") Eula Cooper – 'Let Our Love Grow Higher', Johnny Taylor – 'Friday Night', Anderson Brothers – 'I Can See Him Making Love', Detroit Executives – 'Cool Off'.

One time at Wigan, Caesar pointed out these guys who I think were from Birmingham, doing this new dance, which he described as "somebody trying to shake shit off a shoe". I loved it and began to practice at home until I perfected it, wearing a threadbare patch in my bedroom carpet in the process. When I started doing it down the Central, everyone looked at me, but some didn't like the new style.

Fashions started to change too. I was still wearing bags, but I began to notice a few people wearing winkle-pickers, mohair jumpers and stuff like that, and pretty soon adopted the look. It fitted well with a whole funkier type of Northern and the dancing that went with it.

I went to Blackpool Mecca a lot with Ian Muscroft, but he wasn't keen on Wigan and so I didn't get there too often, but when I did, I loved it. One time I'd gone to the Mecca with Ian, Simon Andrews, Steve Caesar and Glen Campbell. We got some cheap digs, had a great night out and crashed there. In the morning we got up for breakfast, feeling a bit worse for wear, and we're all sitting there wondering where Glen was, when in he walks, in a shirt, cravat and smoking jacket! Delusions of grandeur even in those days.

We'd start off at the Central for Northern on Friday nights, but then later plan to go down to the Funk night at Primo's, but often they had to drag me out of the Central because I was lost in the music and wanted to dance to just one more – it was always a rush because Primo's shut at 1pm.

Jill Taylor's story:

I heard a lot of Soul at home from my older brother Geoff, who was a mod and had a nice scooter, and older sister Kath, who went to the Twisted Wheel: Al Green, Sam & Dave, Otis Redding, Edwin Star, Jerry Butler, Geno Washington and the like. When they left home, they left their albums behind in the front room, and I'd play them constantly on an old stereo system.

Me, Jane Barber and Joanne Wilson, old schoolfriends, used to go the Libs in Yeadon, which played all of the popular Soul tunes of the day, Motown and stuff. I think it was Joanne who said she'd heard about this club in town called the Central and suggested we go.

Off we went one Friday night on the bus. We were about 16 at the time and so went straight down there. It was pretty empty, I'm guessing because most were still in the pub, but it soon started filling up. We made our way to the back far-right of the club, a dark corner where we were less conspicuous. We all had a little dance, but we were a bit shy at the time. I think it was Joanne who first pointed you out, maybe she fancied you? Jane used to talk to Arthur Fenn, I'm not sure how she knew him.

As time went on, I became more confident, aided by whisky and Coke, and started dancing more. I particularly liked the stompers, and Patti and the Emblems – 'I'm Gonna Love You A Long Time' was a favourite. We went every week for three or four years, it became part of our lives.

I started going out with you and you introduced me to Cooky and Dave. By this time, I'd stopped wearing the flared skirt Wigan look and had moved onto pencil skirts, Hawaiian shirts, ski pants, mohair jumpers and pointy slingbacks I got from Funny Wonder. I had a pair of Charles Jordan shoes which absolutely crippled me, but I wore them all the time anyway; they were so nice. I'd buy clothes in New York when I went over there to visit my sisters, who'd emigrated in the early 70s. It was fabulous, and I'd go to clubs like Studio 54 and Magique with Kath and her partner Ivor, who had a press pass and got us in for nothing, queue jumping when the queues were miles long and getting free drinks in the private lounges.

The Central changed to Jazz Funk on Fridays and I loved it. The music was brilliant, it was new, and it really appealed to me. The crowd in general were more fun-loving and extravagant dressers than in the Northern days, but many of our old crowd joined us. I remember Oky, Dave Hayes, Eric Smith, Simon and Caesar (when they came up from London). My dress sense changed again: instructed by me, my mum made me silk wraparound dresses from Vogue patterns and I grew my hair long, in a more sophisticated look, but I've got to say my behaviour was far from sophisticated; I'd get very drunk on whisky and Coke, the whisky from a squeezy bottle I smuggled in my handbag. I loved tunes like John Klemmer's 'Brazilia', Lonnie Liston Smith, and did my best to dance to them.

The Central was the place to be, the only place I wanted to go in Leeds. It was a sad day when it closed and we had to move on to places like the Bank and the Warehouse for a while, which played Funk but were no longer exclusively Funk clubs, mixing it with that new romantic stuff I couldn't stand. It was no longer the underground scene we loved.

Jane Barber's story:

The starting point for me was Fieldhead youth club in Guiseley, where they played the Soul and Motown of the day. We got a record player in the 3rd year of school, and Jill brought in Barbara Randolph – 'I've Got A Feeling', and that's when we went dance mad, playing it over and over again and dancing at the front of the classroom, trying to do the Northern Soul shuffle we'd seen at the youth club. After that time, we went to the Libs in Yeadon, where it wasn't all Northern, but Graham Dibb did a spot, and because we danced and others didn't, Northern got more than its fair share of the night. We were 13, and a whisky and Coke cost 15p, those were the days. It was packed, with a lot of people who were into Soul, but not necessarily Northern Soul. I remember tunes like Edwin Star – 'SOS', but then later things like Kim Tolliver – 'I Don't Know What Foot To Dance On'. I can still see Billy Beanland, who was a big lad but very light on his feet, dancing to that. James Fountain, Barbara Mills, and Black Nasty; as Graham's collection grew, the music got better and better.

I heard about the Central from Graham. Jill and Joe got to go before me because I had to be home by 9pm in those days! It wasn't long before I started telling fibs about staying at Joanne's, so I could go with them. We got the bus into town and back again. We'd have a couple of drinks there, but it was all about the music and dancing. Pretty soon we were there every Friday. I think we were 16 at this time and I absolutely loved it, it was like a transition from childhood into adult life in town, with the grown-up soulies who'd been on the scene for years. It seemed so underground and exciting, and we liked that none of our other friends had heard about it.

We'd always stand in the back-right of the club, around a booth and opposite you and your crowd, but we didn't get to know you until that fateful day we all met jumping the train to Wigan when four of us crammed into one toilet.

We got friendly with Martin Scatchard, Chris Simcock and Graham Spink from Harrogate at Wigan, and then we knocked around with them at the Central. Every night was fun down there, and Oky was one of the best dancers, he seemed such a super stylish man at the time, who'd been around on the scene and was very impressive, as was Eric Smith. I remember Oky dancing to Frankie Crocker – 'Ton Of Dynamite', Gil Scott-Heron – 'The Bottle', and French Fries – 'Danse a la Musique'.

Pretty soon we were going to the Precinct before we'd go to the Central, a cool place with a multicultural crowd happily cohabiting. I kept going to the Central right to the end, before I went to Australia in '81.

The Central is where I grew up and found my groove.

Michelle Dudhill's story:

I was about 17 when I started going down, after school days, in around '75. We all used to meet up in the Precinct, and then one night decided to have a look down the club we'd heard about, the Central. Our crowd was Elaine Murphy, Lynne Butler, Denise Thompson, Lynn and Diane Baxendale, mainly old school friends and friends of friends. Diane went out with Steve Cook, which is how I got to know him and his crowd. I'd been into chart music before, so this was my first introduction to Northern Soul. This was the best time for music, all the Motown and chart Soul, but then all this rarer stuff.

Steve Luigi was one of our first contacts down there, introduced to us by Gary Field, who was an old school friend. Gary Field and Lynne Butler dated throughout high school off and on and then married in the early 80s. The atmosphere I remember as being electric but friendly, with that thumping beat: it just felt right and that I belonged. It got to the stage we didn't need to meet up beforehand, you felt comfortable going down on your own, knowing that you would see people you knew there.

Tobi Legend is a tune that has always stayed with me and helped me through hard times, the words fit so many situations. I've still got a lot of records under the bed, I must dust them off, Judy Street, Jimmy Radcliffe, stuff like that. Oky was a good dancer at the Central and later Mally, who was a bit younger. I was OK, but Cheryl was good.

Derek Wood, the old manager and now a neighbour, used to burn me CDs to listen to. I met him again when out walking my newborn daughter 24 years ago and got chatting. He disclosed that he'd just lost his wife, Joan, and how they both used to love dancing, as it turns out at the Central. He was a bit grouchy at the Central back in the day, not surprising having to put up with us lot, but he became a good friend and help to me later in life, a lovely man.

Easter Bank holidays were always a massive event, when all the Leeds and Yorkshire Soul crowd would descend on Scarborough, thousands of scooters, we took over the town. I remember jumping on the back of Cooky's scooter one time, a little tipsy and with no helmet, and being followed by the police, lobbing chips at them, but somehow managing to hang onto the rest of our tea. I don't know how we weren't arrested, but all innocent fun.

The Central and the memories have seen me through some tough times. I'm very happy and independent now, and really enjoying the reunions.

Gary Davison's story (aka Sam):

I've still got all my old membership cards, ones reading "The Central Dance Club" and later "The Central Soul Club".

114

I got into Soul in about '73 through my mate Geoff Dalby from Swillington, his sister and her boyfriend Kev Rylatt from Castleford. I was round at Jeff's, and they came home one Sunday morning, after a night at VaVa's. They had a box of records, and when they went to bed, me and Jeff started playing them, and to this day I can remember them all. I was blown away and thought *right, I'm going to get all of them*, which I did, on pressings initially; things like Frankie and the Classicals, Tempos, In Orbit, The Snake.

In '74 I got *Blues & Soul* and saw the advert for Wigan Casino. I started buying all the tunes that were mentioned on pressings from Jumbo. The first ones were Invitations – 'Skiing In The Snow' and Tony Clark – 'Landslide'. I built a bit of a collection and started DJing at the local youth clubs, Garforth, Swillngton and Kipax, and through that got to know a couple of older guys, one being little Melv Palfreman. We'd take our records into school at that time and play them in art class and a bit of "one-upmanship" started to develop, who had the best and rarest tunes, we were really getting into it.

I started work at John Waddingtons the printers as an apprentice in September '75 and heard about the Central from Jeff and another mate of mine, Ian Hulme; they'd already been going for a month or two. I got my first wage at the end of that month, so off I went down there with them. First, I had to get round my dad, an ex-policeman, and he initially said no, because it had a reputation, but eventually he let me. I was 16 but looked 14, so went straight down and not to the Precinct pub as most others did because I wouldn't have got in. I was learning what was what, reading about what was being played at Wigan in *Blues & Soul*, but it was nothing like what was played at the Central, it was different music. I met David Horner, aka Jack, who also lived in Garforth at the Central, and even then, he had built an incredible collection. I had my high-waister bags on that I'd bought from Class, and platform shoes, I must have looked a right div. The next guy I met was Chris Mallows and I thought he was the business. That night I drank four pints of that awful Webster's Pennine Bitter they served down there, which turned flat the minute you left the bar, in those old-fashioned dimpled glasses. I wasn't a drinker, and Jeff and Ian ended up having to carry me home. They knocked on the kitchen door and just left me there and my mum dragged me in.

After that, I started going every fortnight and then every week on Fridays. I hung around with the Garforth crowd, Paul Rowley and Andy Dean became good friends, but quickly got to know everyone else down there, you, Steve Cook, big Mally, Dave Raby, Sally Anne, Pat. I got a scooter in '78, and that's when I met Trevor Harrison, who told me they were all going to ride up to a lad's house in East End Park, and that turned out to be Mally Meah. Others I remember were Chef, Naomi, Michelle Dudhill (who somehow fell out of the back of my car at the traffic lights on the way to Wigan, but I didn't realise until we were half a mile down the road, but that's another story) and Diane Layton.

April '76 I just knew I had to go to Wigan. Little Mel said he knew a guy who would take us, which was big Mally, who was 6'7" and looked like Jimmy Nail. We got the bus into Leeds and made our way to Belle Isle, where we met them in the Omnibus, and then went to Wigan in the back of a transit van. I was just short of my 17th birthday.

When I got my first car, I started taking Sally Anne to Wigan. Her elder sister Jane used to go to the Torch and knew a printer I worked with, Howard Taylor, who did a bit of DJing, all these things connect. He DJ'd with Fred Ward and Dave Box at Normanton baths, in '70/'71. When I started working in '75, this printer asked me what I'd been up to at the weekend, and I said he wouldn't know, but that I'd been to a club called the Central and then Saturday night I'd been to an all-nighter at Wigan. He said he knew all about it; this was Howard Taylor. He's in Australia now with all the other Northern Soul ex-pats.

Records that stand out for me were all the more modern sounds, things like Skullsnaps –'I'm Your Pimp', Frankie Crocker – 'Tonne

Of Dynamite', Pointer Sisters – 'Send Him Back', Marvin Holmes – 'You'd Better Keep Her', Rimshots – 'Do What You Feel', World Column – 'So Is The Sun', Carstairs – 'Really Does Hurt'. Then there were all the Torch sounds, Edwin Star – 'Time', Vibrations – 'Cause You're Mine' (I remember because my mate, Brian Hartford, would do this ear-splitting massive clap) Mel Britt – 'She'll Come Running Back', Crown Heights Affair – 'Dreaming A Dream', Cameo – 'Find My Way', Hippit – 'Hosanna', Jobell Orchestra – 'Never Gonna Let You Go', Vicky Sue Robinson – 'Turn The Beat Around'. When I went to Wigan, I realised they didn't play that stuff there, it was all the big stompers, Salvadors, Tomangoes and Epitome of Sound, but it was a funkier sound at the Central, most of which you could just go and buy as new releases at Jumbo.

I started collecting records more seriously, things like Mel Britt, Major Lance – 'You Don't Want Me No More' (on an Okeh demo) which I paid £8 for off Soul Bowl in around '77, a lot of money in those days. I bought Eloise Laws – 'Love Factory' and Jeanette Williams – 'All Of A Sudden' at Wigan, and coming back on the train, I got them out of the slim little wooden box I'd made to show someone, and ended up leaving the box on the train! I bought Van Dykes – 'Save My Love For A Rainy Day', but when I got it home, although the label was pristine, the styrene had more splits in it than I don't know what. I also had a Johnny Caswell, but one night as I pulled it out of my box, the girl I had just split up with lunged at me and snapped it in half – she certainly didn't "love me anymore". I got loads off Soul Bowl, particularly when I started working shifts and getting more money, things like Major Lance – 'Investigate', Williams & Watson – 'Too Late', Patti and the Emblems – 'I'm Gonna Love You A Long Time': I've still got them all, and they don't owe me a penny.

On the night of Andy Dean's 18th, we went for a drink in the Precinct and got a bit tipsy. We staggered down to the Central and I went in first. Next minute, he came tumbling down the steps, did a summersault, recovered, and continued walking to the bar.

I looked at Joan and she looked at me, and I just said, "Two please," with a straight face.

Me and Richard Castelow, who goes to all the dos, went to Perth Australia on holiday to hook up with Andy, and we met all the ex-pats from Huddersfield, Bolton, all over and it was the Perth Australians Nationals Weekender. They're all out there; Andy, Howard, loads of them. It was 18 years ago, but we returned a couple of years ago and they all still remembered us.

The Central was the best meeting place ever, it was the next step up from the youth club. I was 16 and I didn't want to go to pubs at that time, and it was the place to meet everyone, the hub. I met so many people there who I have remained close to over the years, people from Wakefield, Horsforth, Belle Isle, Bradford, all over West Yorkshire, it was the catalyst. Facebook has brought us all back together. It's nice to know everyone's still out there and that they are OK. It was a massively important part of our lives and formed what we are.

Mally Meah's story:

I was 14 when I started going down there with Liz and Trevor Harrison; there's a great photo of us, and Trevor has got his school tie on! I got into it through Trevor Hartford and Tony Kewell, who were a lot older. They had a fruit and veg business, and I'd help them load the wagon and work the stalls on Saturdays when I was still at school. They'd be playing Northern Soul all the time and next minute they were taking me to Rudie's, Blackpool Mecca and the Central. Len's wife, Mary, told me to sit in a corner, so no one could see me, in case the police came in.

I was in awe at first, the dancing was fantastic, and everyone was friendly and looked after me, I was the youngest there. I met Oky, who I recognised from my street in Hyde Park, and we became friends. He was always battling down there with drunks that strayed in looking for trouble, they were drawn to him like a magnet. There were some other fantastic people I remember; Liz (with her baggy trousers), Trevor Harrison, Andy Dean, Matty Sherlock and Gary Davison (Sam).

It was always kicking off. It was in a rough part of town, with notorious pubs like the Star and Garter, the Whip, the Peel, and the drunks would wander down to the Central at kicking out time. I'd stay out of the way in the corner.

My favourite records from those days were The Carstairs, Mel Britt, James Fountain. Later I remember Pat Brady playing Billy Hambric – 'She Said Goodbye'. I got on with Ian and Swish, they'd always have a chat and try and play what I asked for if they had it, but Pat was a bit more guarded at the time, he used to cover up his records. I'd carry Ian's records when we went to Cleethorpes, that way I'd get in for nothing. He had a house in Harehills, with two cellars stacked full of vinyl.

All the top DJs have played the Central; I remember Richard Searling and Kev Roberts doing a spot, I think at the all-dayer in '78, and I heard Chris King play there.

Ian and Paul Schofield inspired me; they were fantastic DJs and really nice people, breaking brand-new records, I learnt from them. I loved things like War, Galaxy, and one of my favourites, A Taste of Honey – 'Boogie Oogie', Hi Tension, O'Jays – 'I Love Music', which is my favourite record of all time. Then there was all the Jazz Funk stuff; Azymuth – 'Jazz Carnival', Lonnie Liston Smith – 'Expansion'.

Going to the Central made me, it changed my life. I was only 14 and Northern Soul was everything, and although I went everywhere, Wigan, Cleethorpes, the Central was the place for me, the main focal point, because of the DJs and what they played and the people; I still have many of the same friends from those days. You've got to keep smiling, even through the hard times, and I have great memories of my time there.

Gip Dammone's story:

I was not really into Northern Soul and only went to the Central a couple of times, but I know guys like Pete Dillon and Derek Barnett, who are a couple of years older than me, who would frequent the Blue Gardinia, otherwise known as the Bee-Gee, which was my dad's old place. There was a big coffee bar scene in Leeds at the time. My dad, Salvo, had come from southern Italy in the 60s and had the café, an Italian style coffee shop, serving frothy coffee in Pyrex cups, just off Boar Lane. Above the café there was allegedly an illegal casino, and the club was in the basement, so the whole building had a bit of an edge to it.

The Bee-Gee attracted the mods back in the day, who decamped from the Conque d'Or or the Conk as it was known and hosted some amazing artists; Long John Baldry with Rod Stewart and Brian Auger, Joe Cocker (who had to get straight off after his spot to get back to Sheffield, because he was on the night shift on the buses) and, I believe, the Four Tops amongst others.

Much, much later the place became a trendy restaurant called Home, with a little exclusive club downstairs, and knowing one of the owners, who also did a bit of band promotion, I was asked to help with some promotion work for it. He was staggered when over dinner one night I told him my dad had owned the place, and some of the big-name acts he'd put on. The then owner wanted to put Giles Peterson on, and had rung his agent, who referred him to me because Giles would only do stuff in Leeds through me at the time, but I assured him Giles wouldn't like the place anyway. I suggested putting on some smooth Soul and Jazz Funk, but then he got fixated about putting some Northern Soul on. Long story short I ended up getting Richard Searling to DJ, he and Judith having a lovely meal before he DJ'd, but the Northern Soul crowd were gobsmacked by the price of the fancy drinks, and they all kept nipping out over the road to the pub, having a pint and then coming back. Needless to say, it didn't work as a Northern night; it was too posh.

I was a suedehead in my young teens, into Tamla and Reggae, with pretend sideboards, but the older lads who went to the Conk (which was by this time called Lulu's) had real ones, they had a bit of a hard rep and we looked up to them.

Dad opened a few cafes besides the Bee-Gee – the Unicorn in Stanningley, frequented by greasers, and Gino's on Kirkstall road. We moved back to Italy in the early 70s for a few years, then he came back and established Salvo's Italian restaurant in Headingley, which we've expanded and remains extremely popular to this day.

My accidental connection to the Northern scene was also through Tony Banks and his famous record collection. A mate of mine had an auction house, and whenever a record collection came in, I had asked him to contact me so I could have a look at it. When Tony died, my mate called me up and told me that he'd got a load of records, along with all sorts of other crazy stuff, that the guy was a true "Womble", a real collector. I asked him to name a few of the labels, and I then realised this was a big find and told him I'd be round the next day. There were piles of beautifully made wooden boxes, and I asked if I could put an offer in for the lot. He said he would put the proposition to Tony's widow, which he did, and she accepted. When I started going through it all, it became apparent there must have been another box, as there were some sequential numbers missing from the collection, the golden box, I'm guessing with all the super rare stuff that wasn't there. I asked my mate the auctioneer if there were any more, and then he told me that he'd been over to the house, and amongst other things were two pristine condition vintage Tucker American cars, the rare ones with the single headlamp that moved on rotation of the wheel, loads of toy cars in boxes, it was a massive sale. He talked to Tony's widow and got to the bottom of the missing box: one of Tony's mates had kept coming around pestering her, saying that Tony had promised him some records, and eventually she'd given the special box to him.

I listened to every record, a few thousand, up in the spare room above the restaurant, but it was mostly classic golden age Northern, not really my bag; I'm more into the more modern, jazzier side of things. I kept a bunch for myself though, the ones I liked plus some of the Northern stompers, things like Ray Charles – 'I Don't Need No Doctor', Gene Chandler – 'There Was A Time', Vibrations – 'Cause Your Mine', Case of Time –'Manifesto', Johny Sayles – 'Can't Get Enough', Carstairs, Leslie Uggams, James & Bobby Purify – 'Shake A Tail Feather', Jewels – 'We've Got Togetherness', all the Kent compilations. As for the rest, I was opening a new shop, and I effectively exchanged shop fitting for records with Gary Fields. My wife probably wouldn't have appreciated all them records coming home anyway, my house is already overflowing with them, but boy do I wish I'd kept more.

In the 80s we had a restaurant called the Coconut Grove with a club in the basement, and the resident DJ was old Northern boy Steve Luigi. I also met the author of this book, Steve T, as part of a crew who promoted a night called Downbeat there, with rare groove in one room and more modern club sounds with Nightmares on Wax in the other.

As a club promoter from the 80s onwards, I would occasionally see some of the old Northern boys at our gigs, which included Terry Callier, Weldon Irvine, Gil Scott-Heron, Lee Fields, Mark Murphy, Jimmy Smith, Rueben Wilson, Roy Ayers, Carleen Anderson, Sharon Jones, Charles Bradley New Mastersounds and the like.

Now I think about it, I have more connections with the Northern scene than I ever imagined!

Steve Walwyn's story:

From my early teens my family and friends were mostly into Reggae and Ska music, that's all I heard at the time. I started going to the Mecca and the Precinct, which were popular venues in Leeds, that's where I got into Soul music.

I was listening to the Emperor Rosko show on Radio One, and he mentioned that the Torch was closing down. I was intrigued. I knew the Central played Northern Soul and went there the following weekend to their "last night at the Torch" night. I went with a friend of mine called Rod Gooding. The atmosphere was electric, and the music was unlike anything that l had heard. From then on l started going to Northern Soul clubs up and down the country, including Wigan Casino and Blackpool Mecca, with friends from Leeds and Harrogate, including Spenner, Lynne Cervi and Andy Wilson to name but a few.

In my late teens, l had moved away from the Northern scene and started going to clubs like Primo's, which had a more culturally diverse crowd, where Paul Schofield was playing Jazz Funk and Soul. Later we started going to London, to places like Ronnie Scott's, Crackers, The Wagg, Global Village and Rafters in Manchester. Then Paul Schofield and Ian Dewhurst started playing at the Central, which was light years ahead of anywhere else in terms of the music. Almost every week there were new releases or something new to hear, which made it exciting. Ian eventually went on to be resident DJ at the Warehouse, and although he played some Soul and Funk, he was playing lots of other stuff like Grace Jones, Joy Division and New Order, mixing it all together. The Warehouse became more of a place to be seen and to socialise rather than Soul music.

I've gone full circle, l have a 1964 Lambretta and am back into Northern Soul. I DJ these days at Moortown Soul Club, run by Diane Layton and Andy Carling, along with a few other venues. I've created an event called Bohemia in Leeds with my brother Mike Walwyn, who DJ'd at the Central under the Liquid and HiFi Club brands. Mike created The Harlem Bush Club and Boogaloo. At Bohemia, along with Mark Warner, Shaun Cottle and Mally Meah, we try and play progressively, bringing people along, incorporating Jazz, Latin, Motown, Northern and Modern Soul.

The concept works and it's bringing in a younger and diverse crowd, which I feel is important.

The Central for me is where it started, being amongst likeminded people, our meeting place, where it was respectful and hassle free, we all loved the same thing: the music.

Diane Layton's story:

I veered towards Soul music in my teens, I wasn't really a pop person; it was always the Isley Brothers, Harold Melvin, Al Green, Detroit Spinners, the well-known Soul acts of the time.

I went to the youth clubs at Benton Park and Stanhope Drive, which played popular Soul, and then I progressed to the Liberal club in Yeadon. My boyfriend and I would take a box of Soul records to play, and this seemed to convert quite a few of the people into Northern Soul. The Cow and Calf in Ilkley was also a regular haunt, where a young Pat Brady DJ'd on Sundays, which was more Northern. I remember there was a couple of steps up to the DJ booth, with a window which I would knock on to make requests, that's how I got to know Pat.

I was around 15 in '73 and out with my mates in town when a lad who one of the girls knew, who was a bit older than us and carrying a box of Northern Soul records, approached us and got chatting and told us about the Central. We had heard about the club from some of the older Horsforth lads also, who'd started going. One weekend we decided to give it a try and a group of us went down. That first time was great; a small club but with a great atmosphere and music. I was surprised how many people there I actually knew, a lot from Horsforth and Pudsey. I loved it instantly, and it became a big part of my life, my week spent looking forward to the weekends and the Central.

Some of my girlfriends eventually drifted away, they were more into the pub scene, the Precinct and the Old Ball, but I wasn't a big drinker and just loved the music and dancing. In 1975 I met Jeff Leighton, a few years older than me and already a regular Central goer, and I then started going down to the club with Jeff. We had a great bunch of friends there, Sam and Jacqui, Fritz and Yvonne, Andy Hudson, John Sheffield (Shef), Keith Layton, to name a few. I had passed my driving test at this point, so my little blue Mini took us all over at the weekends, Wigan, Cleethorpes, Ritz Manchester, Samantha's Sheffield, Raquel's, plus Scarborough at the Bank Holidays. At the Central I would park up at the Corn exchange, and twice got my car stolen from there!

At the Central, we would sit in the alcove at the top side, away from the DJ booth. I never went drinking beforehand, I wasn't interested and had itchy feet, I just wanted to be there dancing. Tony Banks briefly, Paul Rowan, Swish, Frank and then later Pat. Frank was my favourite, I just loved what he played, he was very forward thinking, and the 70s stuff he played still sounds fresh today. I followed him to Cleethorpes, which was probably my second favourite venue.

In 1977, Jeff and I split up, and I made friends with Liz Turner from Horsforth, who was the best female dancer there; she had really fast feet and could compete with the men, she was mesmerising to watch. I also became friends with Sue Davison, Gary's sister, and I continued going to various venues with them. In addition, I had a lot of friends from Harrogate, John Horner and David Roach to name but two. They would pick me up in Horsforth and we'd all go down to the Central. Happy days.

So many Central tunes to choose from, but some of my favourites were World Column – 'So Is The Sun'; I can remember Oky dancing to it, he was one of the best dancers down there, such a good stomper. Eloise Laws – 'Love factory', a massive Central sound, Anderson Brothers – 'I Can See Him Making Love To You', a great Frank spin. In the early days Jimmy Radcliffe was played as the last record, the lights would come on and couples would have a bit of a smooch.

I went to a few of the Jazz Funk nights at the Central and quite enjoyed it, but it was very different, and I stayed mainly with the Northern Soul.

Some of my Central memories include all the smoking in the club. We forget that now, but my clothes would stink after a night out, my mum was always telling me off. Combined with the talc on the floor, it was pretty unhealthy looking back. It was so small, packed and a bit claustrophobic, sweat and condensation dripping from the roof. The toilets were not nice and often flooded.

Throughout the years I have never stopped going to Northern Soul venues. Through the 80s, places like the Carlton club and the Manhattan Harrogate. 90s I moved to Rotherham and went to all the clubs around there, Pitches, Phoenix club, Canklow, but I'd still come back up for Brighouse and Wilton Ballroom.

My partner and I hosted a couple of venues in Selby, Abbey Leisure and the Football club in Selby, which continued for about three years. I enjoyed DJing and playing my records out.

Moving on to the 2000s, I co-promoted a Modern Soul & 70s night in Calverley Leeds, something a bit different, and also ran a club in Haworth. Present day, I co-promote Moortown Soul Club with Andy Carling, where we play a broader spectrum, Northern, Modern, Crossover. It's been going for about four years now, and we also do gigs at the Wetherby Engine Shed and Tadcaster Riley Smith Hall. I feel I'm forever printing flyers and booking DJs!

To sum up, the Central was my life back in the 70s, I'd live for the weekends. I eventually knew most of the people there and I cried when it closed. It's still to this day my favourite venue, and I've been to many. The music, the dancing, the friendships, the DJs; a little club but full of life and atmosphere.

Who would have thought a young 16-year-old girl who loved the Central and the music it brought to her would be DJing with Pat

Brady some 47 years later at the Wardrobe and working with Frank as a guest DJ at her own venue?

Hunter Smith's story:

In the early '60s, after I left school, my brother joined a band. I couldn't play any instruments, and so eventually bought a van and would run them about to gigs. I got known for having a van, which by this time I'd upgraded, and so for most of the '60s, up until '69, I was working through the day and being a roadie by night.

One of the main bands I was working with broke up in '68, and at that time I met a DJ who used to do the old Mecca, Pete Brent, and also Mike Royle, who went on to do the new Mecca and Rollerina. They suggested buying the PA equipment from the band, getting a couple of decks and starting to do some mobile work, which is what we did in '69/'70. We called it Jumbo Mobile Discotheque, using the elephant symbol we ultimately used for the shop.

After a few weeks it got so busy I had to start DJing as well, as they were doing the nights at the Mecca, and so I had to do all the pub work. My DJing was getting better, and they were introducing me to Soul music, and then eventually I also got a job at the Mecca, doing Monday or Tuesday nights. There was another guy called Rick Vaughen, he was a big Soul DJ, and of course Tony Newton (or Tony Banks as he called himself, presumably after Homer) who had an amazing collection. Tony also had a van in the early 60s, running bands around, in fact I think I took one of his bands off him. He was really into his sounds but didn't seem to take a lot of notice that was going on around him. The Mecca manager was a guy called Tony Marshall, who eventually became an MD for Mecca. He started at the Old Mecca and then went onto the Cats Whiskers in Meanwood and was instrumental in the Leeds club scene at that time.

I fell into the shop business completely by chance. An acquaintance asked me if I wanted to sell records in the back of his shop, which was selling tape cassettes and equipment in the Merrion Centre in '71. Within three months, he wanted the space back, so I tramped the streets of Leeds to find new premises. I found a great little place on the balcony of the Queens Arcade, and in January '72 we moved in. There was no initial plan for the shop, it just seemed and good idea and it grew from there. It was a bit of a hobby initially, my main income coming from the DJing.

The shop became a major hangout for the Soul and Reggae crowd, it would be busy most days, but packed on Saturdays, when the Northern Soul crowd would descend on the shop and outside on the balcony. Guys like Pete Dillon, Dave Maltas, Steve Caesar and Swish, chewing gum and discussing the reviews from *Blues & Soul*, tracking the records down and planning their trips to Wigan and places like that.

By this time, I was heavily into Soul and buying it for the shop, and at the same time doing two nights at the Mecca, downstairs in the Merrion Centre, and also on Thursday nights at Samantha's upstairs, which was also part of the Mecca. I'd play all Soul, Funk and Reggae, and attracted a large black following, but the Mecca were always kicking off that the bar takings were down because the guys were dancing instead of buying drinks. They tried to get me to stop playing black music, and the bouncers on the door had clickers, actually counting the number of black people going in, but I refused to change. Eventually I got sacked and went back to doing mobile work. By this time, we had outgrown the shop on the balcony, and so in '74 we moved to new premises at the top end of the Merrion Centre.

I still had the van and did a lot of work at the colleges, the polytechnic and university. There was a group of Nigerian students who organised the Grand Funk Society, and every 2nd week they had a do in the refectory, and we'd absolutely fill it, playing Soul and Reggae, all the latest stuff, I got all the imports from Jamaica and the US. I did also play what might now be termed Northern Soul at Wakefield Mecca on Saturday nights. The shop continued to grow, and Ian Dewhirst and Paul Schofield became big customers, Paul often buying a whole album for just one track to play down at the Central Jazz Funk nights.

I carried on the mobile work until about '80, but it was hard work lugging all the gear around, setting it up, DJing and then packing it all up at 2pm and taking it home. It was taking its toll. At the same times the shop was a hell of a lot busier, and so I sold all my gear and focused on the shop. It had really boomed in the mid-seventies when punk came in, as the punks liked Reggae and that was one of our specialities.

I never personally made it to the Central, I was busy with other things, but knew a lot of guys who did, and was supplying many of them with records. It's nice to have been part of the jigsaw.

CHAPTER 7

THE CROSSOVER YEARS

The three-day week and blackouts had ended, Ted Heath was ousted, and Harold Wilson elected as prime minister, a Yorkshireman. Perhaps more importantly for us, Leeds United had been crowned first division champions for the second time in the '73/'74 season, with the legendary squad of David Harvey, Terry Cooper, Paul Madely, Gordon McQueen (big Jack Charlton had just retired from playing, as had Johnny Giles) Paul "Speedy" Reaney, Norman "Bites Your Legs" Hunter, Billy Bremner, Eddie "The Last Waltz" Grey, Mick Jones, Alan "Sniffer" Clarke, Peter "Hot Shot" Lorimer, Terry Yorath, Joe Jordan, Trevor Cherry and Mick Bates. Contrary to the disrespectful and disingenuous "dirty Leeds" tag, dreamt up by the envious, this was Super Leeds, the team lining up before kick-off to wave to the crowd and kick autographed footballs into it, stringing 70 to 80 passes together at a time with the crowd rewarding each one with an "Ole", before engaging with the fans yet again at the end of the game to hand out autographed stocking tabs to those lucky enough to grab one. Halcyon days, and the city was full of energy and confidence, which reflected in the music at the Central.

The beats were getting a little funkier and more complex, the dancing more stepping on the spot rather than shuffling side to side, and for me I was having even more fun and didn't have a care in the world other than the scene. Was it because I was a bit older and more self-confident, or was it because the music was more optimistic and forward-looking, reflecting the apparent progress in civil rights in America and the emboldenment of 70s Soul Power, coupled with a belief that here in Britain in that period before the Thatcher era, we had the world at our feet and could be whatever we wanted to be?

These are some of the tunes I recall from those crossover days:

- Carstairs – It Really Does Hurt Me
- Detroit executives – Cool Off
- Frankie Crocker – Ton Of Dynamite
- Montclairs – Hung Up On Your Love
- World column – So Is The Sun
- Anderson Brothers – I Can See Him Making Love
- Harold Melvin – Get Out
- Gill Scot Heron – The Bottle
- Larry Saunders – On The Real Side
- Oscar Perry – I Got What You Need
- Ann Sexton – You've Been Gone Too Long
- Bobby Franklin – Ladies Choice
- Paul Humphrey – Cochise
- Moments – Need To Be With You
- Chuck Jackson – Need To Be With You
- Kenny Smith – Lords What's Happening
- Bobby Hutton – Lend A Hand
- Skullsnaps – I'm Your Pimp, My Hang Up Is You
- Joe Hicks – Don't It Make You Feel Funky
- Lou Edwards – Talking About Poor Folks
- High Voltage – Country Road
- Jo Amstead – I've Got The Vibes
- Jesse Fisher – You're Not Loving A Beginner
- Raw Soul – The Gig
- Dianne Jenkins – I Need You
- Elouise Laws – Love Factory
- Kenya Collins – Love Bandit
- Millie Jackson – House For Sale
- First Choice – This Is The House
- Major Harris – Call Me Tomorrow
- Sister Sledge – Don't You Go Through No changes
- Betty Wright – Where Is The Love

- Earth Wind and Fire – Happy Feelings
- Esther Phillips – What A Difference A Day Makes
- George Benson – Supership
- East coast connection – Summer In The Parks
- Nanette Workman – Lady Marmalade

At the same time, more traditional Northern tunes were still breaking, such as the Yum Yums – 'Big Thing' and the Jades – 'I'm Where It's At'.

On a personal note, some of these tunes introduced me to albums for the first time (for example, Millie Jackson, Betty Wright, Earth Wind and Fire, Skullsnaps and Major Harris), and as I played and listened to the whole thing, not just the big tracks, I began to appreciate the wonderful breadth of Soul music. It was the start of a musical journey and a lifelong love of the spectrum of Black Music that continues to this day, not just that stomping 4x4 beat of the early Northern tracks, albeit I still love them, and they are engrained in my heart.

Later still the beats had an increasingly commercial sound, and some of the records were even creeping into the mainstream charts. We wouldn't have acknowledged it at the time, but this was disco, a phenomenon that was sweeping all the major clubs in the western world and ultimately popularised by John Travolta's *Saturday Night Fever*. This was not pop disco though, this was our disco, soulful and obscure and often made by the same artists that we had grown to love over the years, artists who needed to eat and had got with the programme. Just as with the 4x4 Soul that had preceded it, there was an explosion in the production of this sound, cut in small quantities on local independent labels by young black Americans across the US, and quickly deleted due to lack of widespread sales. Once again, years after the event this led to a goldmine of rare and highly collectable 45s, now being played and discovered on the Modern Soul scene, with some commanding incredible prices.

Some of the more popular Central tunes from that era, most of which were relatively easy to get your hands on at the time, were:

- Rimshots – Do What You Feel
- Fat Larry's band – Centre City
- Tramps – Hold Back The Night
- Kim Tolliver – I Don't Know What Foot To Dance On
- Archie Bell – Soul City Walking
- Dells – Your Song
- Roger Collins – Sexy Sugar Plum
- Willie J and Co – Boogie With Your Baby
- Tramps – Disco Inferno
- O'Jays – I Love Music
- Tavares – It Only Takes A Minute Girl
- Phyllis Hyman – You Know How To Love Me
- Alfie Davidson – Love Is A Serious Business
- Flaming Embers – Have Some Everybody
- Velvet Hammer – Happy
- Master plan – Dance All Night
- Flame 'n Kings – Oh Happy Day
- Black Nasty – Cut Your Motor Off
- Cameo – Find My Way
- Dooley Silverspoon – Game Players
- Ronnie Love – Lets Make Love

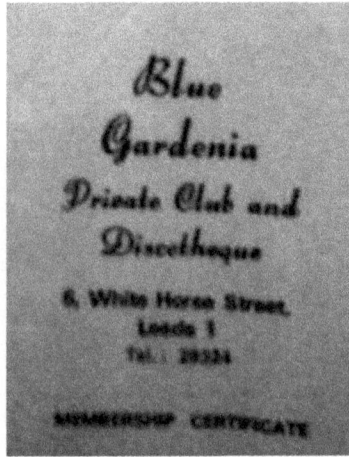

Derek T Barnett's membership cards

Derek T Barnett and Daz near the the salon

Pete Dillon's Hernies membership

Jumbo Records, Queens Arcade balcony

Hunter and customers

Hunter and Lornette busy in the shop

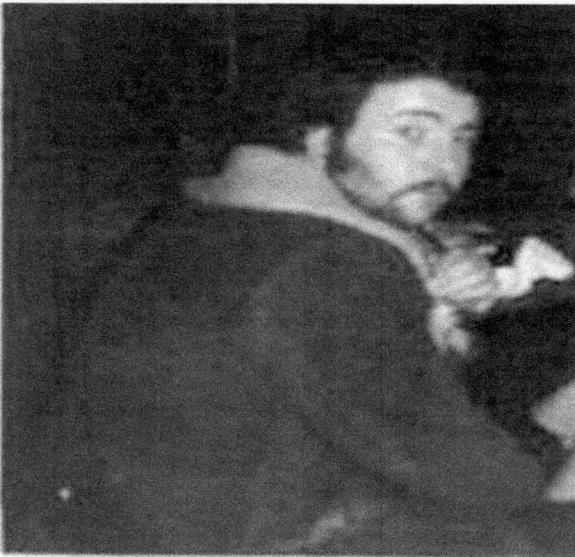

Pete Dillon at the Central

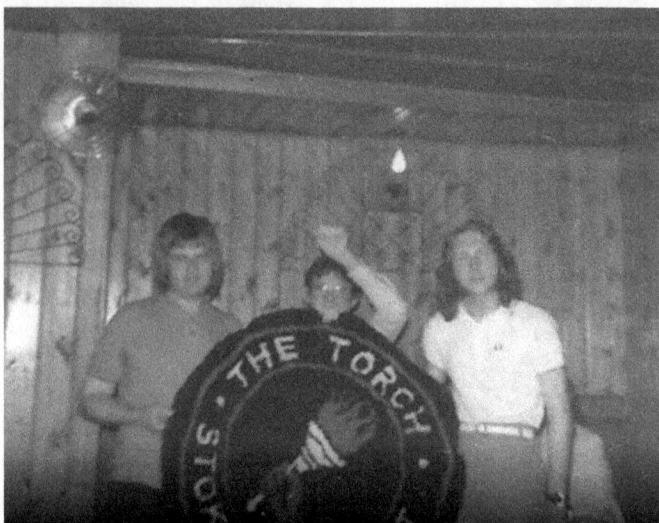

Keith Atkinson, a big Torch badge, Steve Luigi and Dave Maltas

Steve Luigi, Chris Mallows and Paul Rowan

Pete Dillon (second from right) and friends

Eric Smith (Saynor)

Steve Caesar, Dave Maltas, Pete Dillon, Chris Mallows and friends

Steve Caesar, Steve Luigi and friends

Jean Smith and friends

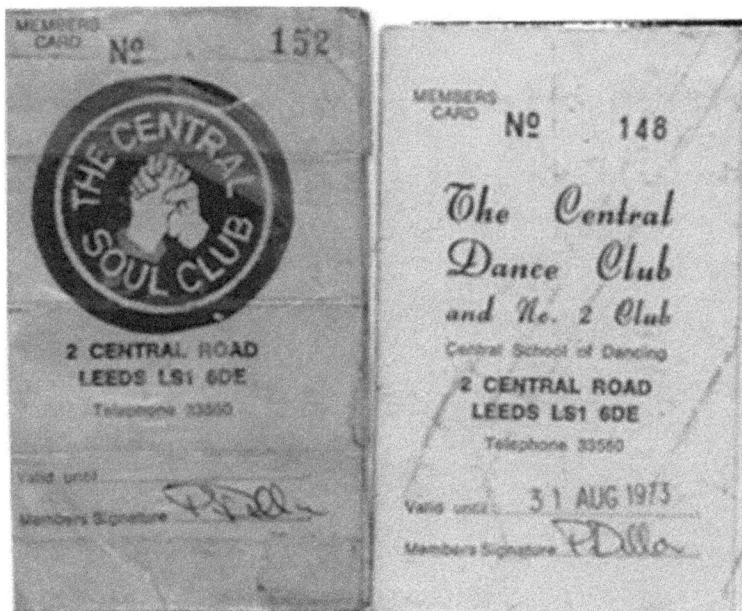

Pete Dillon's early membership cards

Early flyer

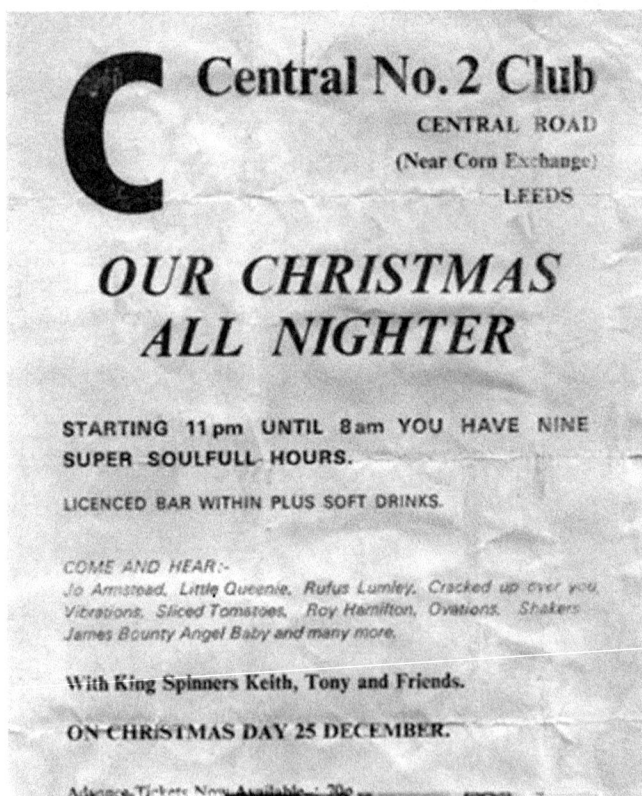

Christmas all-nighter flyer

70 held in drug raid on all-night disco

Yorkshire Post Reporter

SEVENTY people were arrested in central Leeds early yesterday after a raid on an all-night discotheque by members of the Leeds City Police Drug Squad, assisted by members of the West Yorkshire Police Drug Squad.

A statement issued by the head of Leeds CID, Det. Chief Supt. Denis Hoban, late last night said: "Certain substances were seized, and are being examined at Home Office forensic-science laboratories."

Those taken into custody were bailed. They will appear in court on a date yet to be fixed.

The raid was led by Det. Insp. Peter McKay.

The carefully-planned raid was carried out at the Central Dancing School, the entrance of which is in an arcade off Duncan Street.

More than 30 policemen went to the basement discotheque.

It contained more than 140 people, nearly all aged between 18 and 21. They had intended to stay for five and a half hours more, until nine a.m.

Many of the arrested were from outside the Leeds area. A number had travelled from distant parts of the country, including the South of England.

Yorkshire Evening Post press cutting

Pat Brady, Dave Raby, Debbie, me

Early *Black Echoes* ad for Jazz Funk night

Raucous Jazz Funk nights

Queues outside for Jazz Funk night

Dave Hayes, Dave, Jill, me, Annette, Linda

Oky, me (I think Oky stood on my foot) Glen, Dave, Cooky

AT LAST WE'RE BACK!
AND SOUL BREATHES AGAIN!

PAUL SCHOFIELD
AND
IAN 'FRANK' DEWHIRST
RETURN

100% FUNK and DISCO

Outrageous Dress
welcome!

Free Records
on First Night

EVERY FRIDAY
'TIL 2.00 a.m.

THE
CENTRAL

2 CENTRAL ROAD, LEEDS 1.

Licensed Bar and Food available
COMMENCING FRIDAY, 18th NOVEMBER

This will be Yorkshire's No. 1 Funk and Disco
Club. Make sure you come early and don't
miss out on the Latest, Greatest Sounds.

Ian and Paul in full flow, but not a lot else

CHAPTER 8

THE JAZZ FUNK YEARS

❀

The music on the Northern scene had begun to splinter and divide. On one hand, there remained those devoted to the old 60s stompers, and on the other, those enjoying the modernistic funkier and disco beats of the new releases. This modernistic trend was championed by Ian Levine and Colin Curtis at Blackpool Mecca, which ultimately adopted a "new release only" policy, and also by Paul Schofield at Primos, with Frank playing a selection at the Central. Sadly, I only managed to visit the Mecca a few times due to lack of transport and facing the prospect of being stranded in Blackpool at 2am with no money or place to go, unlike Wigan Casino, where I could travel to and fro courtesy of British Rail. Wigan, where I was a weekly attendee from '74 until '79, had lost the plot and lost its Soul in my view, with the exception of Richard Searling who continued to play fabulously soulful tunes, many with a disco beat. Most of the other DJs there opted to stick to the 100mph 4x4 beat, but in their search for rarity with records increasingly by white pop artists. In my view the clue is in the title – it's Northern "Soul" and these records didn't have any. I was losing interest and became frustrated with the music and some of the divs it was now attracting. It was time to move on.

The Central Jazz Funk nights had just started with Paul and Ian in residence, when myself, Dave, Cooky and Jill decided to take a look. I dressed in some of my funkier clothes, encouraged by Jill, who has always loved fashion and had an eye for it, and who was already wearing Hawaiian shirts, ski pants, mohair jumpers and feathered earrings even in the Northern days. We met as usual in the Precinct and had a few drinks to give us a bit of Dutch courage. Around 10pm, we made our way to the club we knew so well, but for a night of music we didn't. As we entered, the music blared and the heat from the dancers hit us, the place was already rocking.

The most obvious difference with the Northern nights was the crowd; the Northern scene was predominantly white, whereas the Jazz Funk night was much more diverse. We made our way to the bar and then drinks in hand cautiously to the spot we occupied for Northern nights, which by this time was nearer the DJ stand, as presumably our dancing abilities and confidence had grown over the years. Some of the music had a soulful familiarity and might these days be called Modern Soul, such as Besse Banks – 'Don't You Worry Baby' played by Paul and still a favourite of mine (which I ultimately paid too much for to have a white demo in my box, whereas I'm pretty sure Paul has the rarer blue normal copy) Jean Carne – 'Was That All It Was' and Phyllis Hymans – 'You Know How To Love Me', which had also been played in the Northern Soul clubs towards the end of my tenure.

As we settled in, we began to recognise familiar faces; there was Oky, Eric and Ian, who we knew from the Northern days, as well as Sally Anne, Janet and a few others. There were also a few black lads who Cooky and I knew from karate (another lifelong passion of mine, which along with dancing has also contributed to my knees and hips being worse for wear). Slowly and over the weeks and months, we were introduced to friends of friends: Glen Campbell, Richard Minnot, Devon Wenham, Vince Enyori and Dave Hays. Glen, one of my closest friends, highly personable and charismatic with an obsessive love of fashion along with jazz dancing. I'll take the opportunity to proudly point out I was his best man at his wedding when he married Sue, and who has subsequently enjoyed a successful career as a TV presenter. Richard, one of the nicest and most compassionate people you could ever wish to meet and one of the most well read, someone to have intelligent discussions with on a host of subjects. I was also his best man, along with Cooky, when he married Kath. Devon (sadly no longer with us) but again interesting and sociable, with an underlying calmness and a deep, infectious laugh and a love and knowledge of Soul music in all its forms, who wrestled for a large portion of his life with a congenital health problem, but which he never let get him down. Oky, raucous, wild and always highly entertaining, a good Jazz dancer. These people have been my friends throughout, and some are as close as family to me.

The music pounded on, and slowly but surely, I took to the floor, adopting my Northern dance to the slower, funkier beats, with less lateral movement and more stepping on the spot. As I said, this dance has stood me in good stead through the ages. Suddenly the music changed, and the floor cleared a little, and into the centre stepped a handful of lads I had not seen before (I think Doville and Wayne were two of them) while Oky and Glen stood their ground. The music was jazzy and frantic, and the dancing mirrored it, with spins and pirouettes, flailing arms and intricate footwork. Wow, so this was the Jazz part of the Jazz Funk scene!

The tunes were a fusion of Jazz horns, strings and keys and underlying fast and funky rhythms. The more popular ones included:

- Ronnie Laws – Always There
- Azymuth – Jazz Carnival
- John Klemmer – Brazilia
- Lonnie Liston Smith – Expansions
- Teena Marie – Portuguese Lover
- Ramsey Lewis – Spring High
- George Duke – Brazilian Love Affair
- Chick Corea – Central Park
- Roy Ayres – Can't You See Me

Although musically brilliant, most of this stuff was too fast and abstract for me to dance to, and I eased myself back off the floor. I never could really dance to the out and out Jazz tracks, although I have made an attempt over the years, often fuelled by alcohol. Fortunately, this was just one spot in the evening and the music reverted back to the soulful stuff, tunes that included:

- Harold Melvin – Praying
- Odyssey – Native New Yorker
- Roberta Flack & Donny Hathaway – Back Together Again
- Jean Carne – Was That All It Was
- Dexter Wansel – The Sweetest Pain
- Jones Girls – Nights Over Egypt
- Phyllis Hyman – You Know How To Love Me
- Slave – Just A Touch
- Positive Force – We Got The Funk
- Blackbyrds – Rock Creek Park
- Patrice Rushen – Haven't You Heard
- Jean Carne – If You Want To Go Back Baby
- George Benson – The World Is A Ghetto
- Brass Construction – Movin
- Players Association – Turn The Music Up
- Fat Larry's band – Center City
- Melba Moore – Standing Right Here
- Brothers Johnson – Stomp
- Nirada Michael Walden – I Should Have Loved You
- War – The World Is A Ghetto
- David Simmons – Holding Back
- Besse Banks – Don't You Worry Baby
- Tom Browne – Funkin For Jamaica
- Cheryl Lynn – Got To Be Real
- Whispers – And The Beat Goes On
- Gap Band – Get Up And Dance

This stuff was right up my street, infinitely soulful and with a beat I could step along to. I had found my new home and danced all night.

The great thing about the Jazz Funk scene was it was fun! I don't just mean we had a laugh, we always had a laugh wherever and whenever, but there was a lighthearted hedonistic vibe to it, unlike the Northern scene, which although enjoyable and generally friendly, always had a bit of an edge; stick to the rules, dance tight and sharp, don't embarrass yourself on the dancefloor, don't act

153

daft, plus a certain paranoia in some quarters perhaps driven by amphetamines.

The Jazz Funk scene was different; anything went. I grew my hair, as most did, into a long-fringed wedge, but short and neat at the sides. The fashions were cutting edge and flamboyant, some wearing Jazz-influenced zoot suits and spats, some wearing punk-influenced drainpipes, Hawaiian shirts and mohair jumpers, others an updated soulboy style. Personally, I wore the latter. I can remember baggy trousers or jeans that tapered to a narrow ankle (for example Hoofers, of which I had a particularly nice black-and-white dog tooth pair, and Rifle jeans) cap-sleeved T-shirts, long and dangling canvas belts, and moccasins or loafers with a modern twist. (I must digress slightly on the subject of loafers.) At this time, Oky was manager of a trendy shoe shop in town, Sasha. In there were a particularly nice pair of light blue loafers with a spongy black sole. They looked the business, so with hard saved cash and a bit of discount from Oky, I bought a pair. They were absolutely wonderful, that was until the time it rained, when the soles magically turned to ice, to the extent you could not take a step without falling on your arse. I spent one fateful Saturday afternoon clinging to the walls of Leeds, making my way to the bus stop to get home. It turns out Glen and numerous others had the same experience, and we have not forgiven or forgotten Sasha and their "death trap" shoes.

Our joyous Friday nights continued for several years and our friendships and passion and knowledge for the music developed. Our regular crew had grown and now was a merger of old Soul boys and girls and newly acquainted Jazz and Funk fans, and was predominantly made up of me and Jill, Glen, Liz, Oky, Eric, Minnie and Cooky and Dave. The nights became wilder and alcohol-fuelled. Money was too tight to mention, and we augmented a few bought drinks with a squeezy bottle of whisky Jill brought in her handbag to secretly mix with her glass of Coke. Cooky and I took to putting it in our Guinness, an acquired taste to say the least, but it did the trick.

At this time my only means of transport was my scooter, and the spectacle of me and Cooky racing our scooters home with Jill on the back, silk dresses and hair flowing, was a sight to behold. One eventful night I was riding home with Cooky on the back, as I was staying at his. Paul Schofield had introduced the weekly ritual of playing Otis Day – 'Shout', which commanded an incredible response from the crowd, winding down to "shout a little bit softer now, shout a little bit softer now" and then winding back up to "shout a little bit louder now, shout a little bit louder now", before leaping up and waving their hands in the air to "jump up and shout now, everybody shout now". For reasons best known to ourselves, we chose to sing that song all the way home, with me removing my hands from the handlebars for the "hey, hey, hey, hey" bit. There is a very sharp bend as you go through Hunslet and make the right-hand turn to Belle Isle where Cooky lived, and I defy any man or woman to get around that corner again in one piece, with two on a Vespa and no hands on the handlebars. Not one of my prouder moments, but we lived to tell the tale. Quite what 'Shout' had to do with Jazz Funk, I'll leave for Paul to explain, but it certainly worked.

One of the regulars was an old friend from the Northern Soul days, a particularly beautiful and stylish young woman. However, on an almost weekly basis and slightly worse for wear, she managed to fall down the Central steps, making a classic entrance on her backside and often displaying more than she might wish as a result. If you know, you know.

There were lots of other interesting characters. I remember a group of deaf lads, who communicated with us by lip-reading and signing, but they did not let their disability hinder them in a night of dancing and merriment. I'm guessing they felt the thumping vibrations and synchronised with the other dancers.

The warm-up venue had moved on from the run-down Precinct to the cellar of a bistro bar run by a lovely Greek fella, called Shine's bar. Everyone socialised and pre-loaded (as they call it now)

155

before moving down to the Central. Sadly, the bar closed some years later, but it was such a memorable venue that on closing night, Cooky was caught walking with the 8' wooden sign under his arm. If I'm not mistaken, I helped him remove it from high on the wall. Always there to help.

Paul and Ian interestingly ran the nights as a business, sharing the door with the club owners, but jointly investing in their own sound equipment and records.

Ian had been a highly successful and influential Northern Soul DJ, playing all the major venues of the day, later working for several major record companies in promotion and A&R and always championing black music, before ultimately returning to DJing and club promotion.

Paul had a successful business career in the travel industry, along with a strong interest in environmental and social justice issues. He was an early Funk promoter and DJ and had built a strong following from the black community in Leeds and beyond.

Together they formed a formidable team and seized that moment in time.

Paul Schofield's story:

I started DJing in Leeds in 1972 at a club complex called the Pentagon, Primos, at the bottom of Briggate. It had three floors. The bottom floor was a bar, the middle was Primos, and the top floor was called Heavens Above. It was owned by the Pentagon chain and run by two brothers. I had originally started to work in 1969 at Batley Pentagon, which was the first one playing Soul two nights a week. I had always been into Soul, as a mod going back to school days in the mid-60s.

They asked me to move to Leeds to DJ on the middle floor, Primos. I started playing black music on Friday and Saturday nights, and soon it became very busy. The owners told me to stop playing black music because it was attracting the wrong crowd... too many black people, the usual shit that came from club owners, and of course we had the National Front and all that nonsense in those days. Anyway, I kept playing it and kept getting sacked. I was sacked seven times, but each time a week later they would ask me back! The mid-70s could be pretty hairy times, and I got threatened by the NF and had paint-stripper poured over my car, but I was not deterred. I saw my job as a DJ was to entertain people and try and educate them, I had a particular love for black music, and nothing was going to stop me playing it. We were seeing a social change, with integration on a scale not seen before. It was the first time members of the Chapeltown black community started coming into the city centre to a club that would let them in, and I was playing the tunes they wanted to hear. It was a really great crowd, totally interracial, which was highly unusual for the day.

It was about this time I came into contact with a young Ian Dewhirst, who'd occasionally come into the Pentagon in Mirfield. He actually lived in Mirfield, as I did, and he was on the Northern scene, whereas I was into Funk side.

He started coming down to Primos in '74/'75, and at the time I was playing Philly international, Salsoul and starting to get into Jazz Funk in a big way. Ian used to come down on his way to DJ at Cleethorpes or wherever he was DJing on the Northern scene, and we became mates.

By this time, I had done a few Ritz Manchester all-dayers, my first one in September '76. I know Colin is felt to be the Jazz Funk king, but I'm sure he'd acknowledge that I was the first to actually start playing it there.

In the summer of '77 I got sacked by the Pentagon management again. They did all sorts of shit: they tried to block the floors off, they tried to create separate entrances, all to prevent this mixed crowd from coming into contact with the other floors. It was nasty stuff and I'd had enough.

I was working for Thomson Holidays at the time, and I said to Ian, "There's a chance of going to Ibiza, if you want to come, I can get cheap flights, and we can have a 5-star hotel for 50 quid each?" He jumped at the chance. Ibiza at that time wasn't like it is today. There weren't many English people there, it was mainly Italians and French. Off we went, and one night we were sitting in this club listening to the DJ who was brilliant. We always thought we were playing upfront stuff, but this guy was another level. It was there that we decided to set up our own club. I was fed up of being shafted and getting sacked every two minutes and only getting a paltry eight quid a night.

As we started to discuss possible venues in Leeds, Ian told me there was somewhere called the Central, which had been a Northern club but was no longer going. We went down and met Len Cave the owner, and we put a proposition to him where we would put a sound system in, and we'd split the door takings and he'd keep the bar. He agreed.

We had three weeks to get organised, and we opened mid-November '77. I remember standing on the door with Ian at 9pm, having sunk quite a lot of our own money into it on the sound system and advertising, and we were bricking it because there was no one there, but by half past 10 it was ram jammed! The club was apparently supposed to have a limit of around 200, but on peak nights, it felt nearer 600.

On Friday nights, we were the hottest club in the north of England. We had coach trips coming from all over, particularly from the North East. Alex Lowes (who later went on to run the Southport weekenders) used to bring loads down. It just worked; we had the right music, the right people at the right time in the right place. We had a nucleus of funkateers, Caesar, Oky, Glen, Douglas from Manchester and all their cohorts, plus there was this great movement from the Northern scene, guys like yourself, who were getting disillusioned with that scene and discovering a whole new side to black music. It was exciting, it was music, it was fashion. We never had a doorman, you either liked the music or you didn't bother coming in; the crowd looked after themselves. It was one of those places you solely came in for the music. You certainly didn't come in for the décor or air conditioning, although to be fair there was a ceiling fan. I have never played in a club where the atmosphere was so intense; I don't know if it was the low ceiling, or that it was in a cellar or the music, but it was brilliant.

The music scene was incredible at this time. You got this wonderful fusion of the Jazz session players playing on the Soul and Funk tracks, and it was new and exciting. I was coming out of the Funk scene, but also got into this new Jazz Funk hybrid. Ian would play more of the disco boogie stuff. It was amazing when we went record buying together on a Thursday, to Jumbo in Leeds or Spinning in Manchester, we had this ten-second test to listen and say yes, we'll take that. Many of the tracks were on albums that we were ploughing through, and at the end of the day we'd split the records down the middle, Ian would take all the disco and I'd take all the Jazz Funk. We ran the whole thing like a proper business, we both put money in and bought the records from that. We'd buy everything that was coming out that we thought was good. Our record bills in '77/'78 were £120 to £150 per week! Any money we made, yes, we had a great time with it, but most was ploughed back into the records and the business. We loved being on top of the scene. We were buying stuff on Thursday or Friday, playing it Friday at the Central, then going to the Blackpool Mecca on the Saturday and hearing Colin and Ian playing the same things, or to Rafters with John and Colin: we played it before them, which was great fun!

It's difficult to remember all the tunes there were so many, but if you ask me which records meant the most to me, I would start with things like James Brown – 'There Was A Time'. It was one of the first records I got into in '68 and I've played it ever since, for getting on 50 years. Another one that means a lot to me is Jean Carne – 'Was That All It Was', because when it came out, it was totally missed by most.

There's a funny story around this one. Ian was notoriously unreliable for his timekeeping at gigs. We were supposed to be playing at a Blackpool Mecca All-dayer at the Crown Heights Affair gig, and for some reason, Ian had taken all the records with him on the Friday night, and we were playing at the Mecca on Sunday. I had a few records with me, about 20, and he had the rest. I'm in Blackpool and no Ian – and remember no mobile phones in those days! Neil Rushton the promoter came up to me and said the venue had just received a call from Ian, and that he was stuck in a toilet on the M62 at Hartshead Moor and that the door wouldn't open. I said the lying bastard, "He's shagging someone!" Neil said, "Look, will you go on after Crown Heights Affair?" I said, "I will, but I've hardly got any tunes with me, only a few 12s." It was a circular stage, Crown Heights Affair finished, and the stage started rotating round to face the crowd, and I thought fuck it, I'll drop me trousers and put a record on! I did, and the record was Jean Carne, 'Was That All It Was', and the place just fucking erupted!

There were so many stand-out records, Jean Carne, Phyllis Hyman, Roy Ayres, but sadly many have become played-out standards over the years. I always preferred the stuff that wasn't played as much. Besse Banks – 'Don't You Worry Baby' was always a favourite. You and Jill stood near the DJ stand, next to Len's organ (ooer missus) and I could always rely on you two dancing to it. I got it from Jumbo, they only had one copy.

On the Jazz Funk front, in '76 Simon Andrews and Oky had been to Chris Hills place down south, and they came back and said, "You've got to get this track, 'Domello' by Roy Ayres." You could only get these tracks on LP, so I bought it, but the other Roy Ayres track I jumped on was 'Hey, Uh, What You Say Come On'. I actually played it at my first session at the Ritz, and tongue in cheek told the crowd that it would become big on the Northern scene, but I got beer cans and all sorts thrown at me! It was a real melting pot of the Northern fans and Jazz Funk fans, and although some liked both, there was a bit of factional rivalry.

That's how Jazz Funk at the Central started, the rest, for three years, was history. It ended in July '80 when Ian went to the Warehouse. I came back from a holiday in Los Angeles, having left Leroy DJing, and came back with a whole load of promos I'd picked up from all the LA record companies. I was excited with this new stuff and started playing it, but people were just stood looking at me in bewilderment and not dancing. The scene was becoming really fragmented, and so I decided to call time on the Jazz Funk chapter.

Ian Dewhirst's recollections from the time:

Paul's night at Primo had come to an end, I think there was a change of management or something, so we went down to talk to Len, and he agreed to let us do the Friday nights as a Jazz Funk night, and then boom, the Central again became one of the hottest nights in the country, certainly outside London. The Northern nights had fizzled out, but there might have been a time when we did Friday nights and the Northern nights continued for a bit on Saturday.

We'd get coach trips from Manchester, Newcastle, everywhere. It was such a hot steamy cellar; it was kind of wild! Always a great crowd. I remember Oky and his mob, Dave Hayes, Eric and various girls, the Sassoon's crowd; it was quite a fashionable club. Oky was at the shoe shop Sacha, it was all very hip, we had all the movers and shakers there.

Steve Caesar's Jazz Funk story:

I also went to Primos in Leeds on Friday nights. I've always had an eclectic taste in black music, and they were playing Funk down there. I started to do the warm-up sometimes for Paul Schofield at Primos. When the nights stopped there in about '77, Paul moved on to do the Jazz Funk nights at the Central, and so I followed him down there. A lot of the more soulful stuff played at Primos and the Central was being played at Blackpool Mecca, what people are now calling crossover, such as Eddie White, Patrice Rushen. Parliament and Brass Construction were big, and all of the Salsoul stuff.

The Jazz Funk days at the Central were fabulous. The crowd changed, and there would be coaches from Newcastle (organised by Alex Lowes, the founder of the Southport weekenders), Manchester, Bradford, all over. It was a different crowd from the Northern, although many crossed over, people like Simon, Ian, Paul, you and Jill, Oky, Eric. It still had that nice friendly vibe the minute you walked through the door. We'd all meet up in the pubs beforehand.

Memorable tunes for me were Charles Earland, Idris Mohammed, Jean Carne, Phyllis Hyman, Kool and the Gang. I liked the Jazz stuff as well, Donald Byrd – 'Blackbird', which I bought on 7" when it came out, Lonnie Liston Smith. I adjusted easily to the change in dancing the music brought, it just came naturally.

The nights were wild, especially when the Newcastle lot came. How we all fitted in that club I'll never know, and there was only one toilet! You could reach up and touch the ceiling, and the bar was so small with only one person serving. You had to dance on a threepenny bit and spin on a sixpence. Were there any fire regulations in those days?

David Okonofua's Jazz Funk story:

Shortly after both the Northern nights at the Central and the Funk nights at Primo ended, that's when Paul Schofield and Ian Dewhirst set up the Jazz Funk nights at the Central. I'd just got back from Brighton and used to go to the Ritz all-dayers, and all the stuff played there influenced me and I encouraged them to play it at the Central. There was me, Caesar, Ian, Glen, Julie, Eric, Dave Hays, Fitzroy and Trash. Trash was beautiful and lovely; she was from a wealthy family and always had nice cars and would pick me up whenever she saw me in town. Sadly, she died a few years ago. She always loved Herb Ward – 'Strange Change', from the Northern days, which was quite obscure at the time and has become popular more recently.

I was part of getting Ian and Frank to play together, and influenced some of the tunes they played, things like John Handy – 'Hard Work', Blackbyrds – 'Rock Creek Park', George Benson – 'The World Is A Ghetto'. I remember Colin Curtis playing George Benson track at the Mecca and shouting. "You won't hear that at fucking Wigan!" There was a real split in the scene in those days, with the Mecca playing the new release and Wigan sticking to the 60s stompers, although in reality there was a lot of crossover at both venues.

I got into the jazzier tunes and Jazz dancing. There were some great Jazz dancers down the Central, Glen, Wayne and Doville to name a few. The floor would clear, and we used to kind of battle each other. My favourites on the Jazz side were artists like John Klemmer, Roy Ayres, Jimmy Castor bunch, Azymuth, Chic Corea, Lonnie Smith, Jimmy Mcgrith. Many of the top tunes were album tracks and I bought most of them from Jumbo.

Caesar was the most knowledgeable of us. He recognised singers and producers from the Northern days and was up to speed with their newer funkier releases, people like Frankie Beverley, who had the big Northern tune 'If That's What You Wanted' and was now fronting a band called Maze. Tunes that bridged the Northern scene and Jazz Funk scene, things like Idris Muhammad – 'Could Heaven Ever Be Like This' and Silvetti – 'Spring Rain'. Others bands we got into were Parliament, Funkadelic, Brass Construction, Slave and Ohio players.

Willie Hunt, my friend and Savile Row fashion designer, used to organise coach trips over from Manchester, and one of the coach members was another friend Douglas, an outrageously ostentatious character I had met at the Mecca. He used to tell me people on the coach were picking on him, but more I think to drag me into intervening with people he didn't like rather than right any actual wrongdoing. That's how I first met Willie, who says I was always threatening him! Willie's version of events is they got sick of having to divert all the way to Oldham to pick Douglas up, rather than him making the short trip into Manchester. Douglas always used to overindulge and peak very early but then would often be found asleep behind the speakers.

There were loads of us, including Pete (sadly departed) and Lorraine from Manchester, who is an MP now. Stuart Cosgrove (the famed author) would come down, Adele from York, Pam from Manchester, people from all over. We'd get absolutely smashed.

We encouraged Paul to play 'Shout' by Otis Day & The Knights, which is from *Animal House*. We'd seen it at Caistor when we'd gone there with Colin Curtis and Steve Caesar. We used to chant songs made up by Simon Andrews wherever we went, things like "the Leeds crowd always innovate, the others all just imitate". It was funny at the time, but you had to be there.

Glen Campbell's story:

I started going to the Precinct in about '74, a funky town centre pub with a boxing ring like dancefloor in the back. I went there with my mate Nigel Obronson, and the crowd were full-on Soul Train, a lot of big afros, flares, platforms, big lapels. They served the drinks in the front bar. I was only 13 and didn't know what to order, so said I'd have the same as the older bloke in front of me, which turned out to be mild, which was awful, and after a mouthful, left it on the bar. I wasn't there for the drink; it was for the music and the dancing. A lot of James Brown, Ohio Players.

I started going to Primo's, which also played Funk, and I was heading down there one night, passing the back of Woolworth's, when I bumped into Oky and two others, who I didn't know at the time. I was always on my guard going through town because I dressed different to most. I got my girlfriend's mother to taper my trousers by taking in the bottoms, I was inspired by 1950s movies with zoot suits and pointy shoes. Oky asked where I was going and I thought *here we go, they're going to start on me*, so I replied, "What's it got to do with you?" He told me to calm down, that he'd only asked because he liked the way I dressed, and why didn't I join them at the Central, so I did.

I remember standing at the top of the stairs and then descending down into this pulsating, sweaty sauna. I'd been used to 70s discos, with flashing lights and glitter balls, but this was something a lot more basic. Already, at this early hour, there was sweat dripping off the low ceiling onto your clothes. You went in looking great, but you knew by the end of the night you'd be like a drowned rat. The music and dancing were incredible though.

Oky introduced me to Simon, Caesar and Ian, who became lifelong friends. They were five or six years older than me but took me under their wing. They later introduced me to Blackpool Mecca and wherever they were going. The crowd was mixed, with mostly funkateers around the DJ booth, but some older guys at the back who'd been on the Northern scene, which seemed like a far-off dark corner.

I've always been into dancing and I was very fit. The Precinct was all a funky strutting-type dance, whereas at the Central there was a faster leg movement, which had come from the progressive Northern Soul crowd; Oky was great at it. I'd dance from the time I got in to the time I left at 2am, occasionally stopping for a quick drink. It was only later that I became aware some of the crowd were fuelled by other things, it wasn't a drinking place.

Oky lived near to me in Hyde Park, so he'd invite me round to his house through the week to hear records he'd bought. We went in the front room, the best room, where some of the furniture was still covered in plastic to protect it for special occasions, and we'd practice our dancing. We'd be working on moves that went with the music, chest bumps and knee spins, legs flailing everywhere, and from time to time his mum would put her head around the door to ask if we were alright, no doubt wondering what the hell we were doing in there and worrying about her best stuff. He always got the latest tunes, so when Paul played them at the Central, we knew the moves we were going to make and got on it straight away. There was only us that danced like this at the time.

If you look at the dancing, we were inspired by James Brown, which was more frantic, whereas the Northern crowd seemed to be more in the flowing style of Jackie Wilson. You could see this clearly at the Ritz all-dayers in Manchester, where the two styles were evident together under the same roof, on that raised bouncy floor. Oky was frantic, Caesar was fluid, I tried to mix both styles together.

When the Jazz stuff came in around '78/'79, we moved the dancing on again, more artistic and taking influence from the great Jazz dancers of old. Those even younger than me picked up the mantle, but by far the best Jazz dancer was Doville, sadly no longer with us, and his posse tried to follow his lead. Collectively, at places like Blackpool Mecca, they'd call us the Leeds Funkateers. We'd dance down from the Bloomfield, the warm-up venue to the Mecca, like a scene out of *Fame*. The other holidaymakers didn't know what to make of it, and some, particularly revellers down from Glasgow, would take offence at the way we looked, and have a go at what they saw as a bunch of weirdos dressed in winkle-pickers, Hawaiian shirts, mohair jumpers and funky hair. There'd always be some violent scuffles making our way down to the Mecca, and the same going back to your digs after, but we could handle ourselves, much to the shock and surprise of our attackers.

I loved all the Philly stuff and Parliament and Funkadelic, Ohio Players, Brass Construction. I loved the tunes that would build and build, but with a break in them where you could go into spins and jumps, some of the trickier moves. On the Jazz side, I loved John Klemmer, Azymuth, Lonnie Liston.

One particularly memorable night, we all rehearsed for Parliament's Flashlight, actually taking torches down with us to the Central. When the tune came on, we flashed the beams around the room, moving with the rhythm and enthralling the rest of the crowd.

The Central felt like home. I had always felt a bit different from being seven years old, on a different wavelength to family and the people around me. I lived with my gran and so was a bit isolated and separated from my older sister Tony, who lived with my mum. At school, although I was a top sportsman and captain of the first 15, socially and academically it was a nightmare for me due to undiagnosed dyslexia and the stigma of free school meals and donated uniform. At the Central I found likeminded people, and my dress by this time was cutting edge, I felt equal, I felt liberated. There were no barriers, we were all there for the music, and we were as one.

Vince Enyori's story:

I would watch *Top of the Pops*, David Essex, David Bowie and the like, but nobody I could relate to. At the same time, I was hearing my father's Soul and Nigerian High Life music around the home. There were few black people on TV at that time, but slowly but surely, they started appearing, Four Tops, Stevie Wonder and the like, and I realised people who looked like me made great music.

My school was predominantly white, so most were into progressive rock. A handful of my white mates liked Tamla Motown and Soul, and some had older brothers who went to the clubs, Wigan, Samantha's. We started to emulate them, listening to their records and copying their dress, Barathea jackets, Jaytex shirts, loafers, a mod look, and looking for places to go that played black music.

One of the elders was a guy called Toddy, who was a regular at Wigan.

There wasn't much happening in Bradford at the time, and a lot of nightclubs were operating racist door policies as recently as the 1990s. I can only think of one club in Bradford city centre that played black music, the Hole in the Wall, which was frequented by scooter boys and mods. I was very young and so only went there a couple of times, but I think that Andy Simpson, who was a friend of Colin Curtis and Ian Levine, was a regular.

My black friends were into Reggae, and my childhood friend, Andy Williams (sadly no longer with us) had a cousin in the Scorcher Sound System, so we went along to listen to them at Green Lane Youth Club. We also went to blues parties, which were mainly Reggae, but then they'd funk it up with things like Parliament, Fatback Band.

Although I liked some of the music, I wasn't really on the Northern scene, but did go to Samantha's, the Cats Whiskers in Meanwood for the all-dayers, Blackpool Mecca and Ritz Manchester, and enjoyed the funkier tunes. Later we went to Rafters and Angels in Burnley for the Jazz Funk. The Bradford crew followed Ian and Paul on some of the 'Botties Over Britain' tour. I met Oky and Caesar at the Mecca, and they suggested going to the Central for the Jazz Funk nights.

I went across to the Central with Jeff Brown, Johnny Henry (who has sadly passed), Ashley and Frank Mears, and some of the women, such as Karen Barnes, Hillary, Mitzi and Sandra. We'd drive across, but for us black Bradfordians, Leeds always seemed big, hostile and violent. We'd sometimes go to the Precinct first, which was multicultural, but usually straight down to the Central. Skinheads would hang out at the Whip across the road, and on more than one occasion they showered us with bottles, goading us to chase them so they could ambush us. It was horrendous. That would never have happened in Bradford, it wouldn't have been tolerated, they'd be run out of town. I must have been attacked five or six times. I won't name them, but I knew people who were on the Northern scene and involved with the NF, but at the same time would be friendly with me. How does that work?

First impressions of the Central was it was loud, dimly lit, hot and sweaty, and absolutely packed, but with great music. It was one of the few places I felt comfortable in Leeds. Memorable tunes for me were 'Spread Love' – Al Hudson, 'Bourgie Bourgie' – Ashford & Simpson, Double Exposure – '10 Per Cent', 'Native New Yorker', 'You and I' – Rick James, the things Paul played. The one I didn't like was 'Shout', I just didn't get it. We became regulars.

Trash (sadly deceased) would dance outrageously, and there were lots of fashionistas, Oky – intoxicated and wild, he and Glen dancing in leather trousers, Pam and Dave Hayes, Steve Lynch, you and Jill. It was a stylish place, which was a bit pointless because it was so sweaty your clothes would get ruined.

The Central was a piece of the jigsaw for me, a local club playing great music, where you met likeminded people. When it closed, Paul moved to Time and Place in Bradford, and a lot of you Loiners started coming through, and they were also great nights. The bouncer was a guy called Moss who fought karate for England, so there was no trouble there, or if there was it was quickly sorted out.

CHAPTER 9

BACK TO NORTHERN

✿

Paul Schofield recognised that Northern Soul remained popular in some quarters and saw an opportunity to re-establish Northern nights on Saturday at the Central, to run alongside the Friday Jazz Funk night, and develop the business partnership he was in with Ian. They had a discussion with the management, who were only too keen to give it a go due to the success of the Friday nights. Ian and Paul assembled together DJs Twink, Paul Rowan, Swish, and later brought in Pat Brady, who had built a following in other clubs by this time. Paul S himself didn't DJ at these nights, as he had never really been on the Northern scene, although ironically a lot of the stuff he was playing at the Jazz Funk nights was now also being played in the Northern clubs.

Pat had been introduced to John Anderson at Soul Bowl by Ian and became an avid acquirer of the top tunes of the day, things like The Chandlers – 'Your Love Makes Me Lonely', 7th Avenue Aviators – 'You Should O Held On', Paris – 'Sleepless Nights'. The rarity and popularity of these tunes at venues such as Wigan drew back the crowds to the Central, and pretty soon the nights were as popular as ever.

After a couple of successful years, the attendance at the Northern nights once again dwindled. In addition, Ian had been offered the residency at the new, purpose-built New York style disco of the Warehouse, an impressive club for its time with state-of-the-art light and sound. Ian accepted the offer, and as such triggered the end of the Jazz Funk nights in '81, which also meant the end of the Northern nights as their partnership dissolved.

After Len Cave passed away, the club was eventually sold in 2001, and the new owners refurbished the venue and turned it into the HiFi Club, which focused its nights on a young student crowd, but still retained an element of Soul, Funk, House and Hip-Hop.

We all went our separate ways. Our crowd followed Paul Schofield to Time and Place in Bradford, where he continued to play Funk and Jazz Funk. These were great nights with many of the old Central regulars in attendance, but as they tended to be alcohol-fuelled, getting there and more importantly back was always a challenge. We also started going to the Warehouse, which played a broad mix of dance and disco tunes, and as such attracted a much broader crowd, but Ian played just enough Soul and Funk to keep us going back, tunes like Maze – 'Joy and Pain' and Dennis Edwards – 'Don't Look Any Further'.

Later still the Electro Funk and early Rap scene developed with the new and exciting sounds of Rappers Delight, Africa Bambata, Kurtis Blow and the like. This scene never fully grabbed us, though, as the dancing turned to body popping and breakdancing, a whole different game that bore little resemblance to our style of dancing, but it kept us entertained until something bigger came along. That something bigger was Hip-Hop and House. I know most of the Northern fans will have thrown the book down in disgust at this point, but bear with me, I'll get through this bit as fast as I can, but for me and most of our crowd this was a musical explosion of similar magnitude to when we first got into Soul. Hip-Hop was a continuation of Funk, using break beats from old Funk records, and we loved its raw energy and strong political and social commentary, with tunes from the likes of Eric B & Rakim, Just Ice, Public Enemy, Ice T and Ice Cube. House was Soul with gospel-tinged vocals the strength of Aretha's or Otis's (but perhaps not quite the quality) from the likes of Byron Stingley and 10 City, Marshal Jefferson, Ce Ce Rogers, Blaze and many more. It was a continuum of soulful disco, and the beats were driving and hypnotic, the dancing fast and energetic. Early soulful House is not to be confused with the Acid House and e-head culture that followed, which sadly lost its Soul; this was tailormade for old Soul boys and girls like us, who loved to dance all night in ecstasy to the pounding beats.

We travelled to the House and Hip-Hop venues around the country, London and Nottingham in particular as there was nothing happening in Leeds at the time, but eventually, and as a result, four of us decided to form a club night called "Downbeat". We started at Bali Hai with a simple formula whereby we took the door, and the club took the bar; the venue had nothing to lose, as it was dead before we started. Flyers were crudely drawn, printed on works photocopiers and distributed around Leeds, and we were in business. I played the Soul, Funk and Swing-Beat (a fabulous hybrid of Soul and Hip-Hop, produced by the likes of Teddy Riley) Mark Kelly played Funk and Jazz, George Evelyn (aka DJ E.A.S.E.) played the Hip-Hop and Kevin Harper (aka Boy Wonder) played House. I was in my mid-late twenties at the time, and some wit nicknamed me Daddy T as I was a lot older than George and Kevin, who were only about 16, a name that stuck with me for a while. Pretty quickly we built crowds of up to 500, by which time the management got greedy and begrudged handing over the money, thinking they could do it themselves for next to nothing. They kicked us out, replacing us with cheap clueless DJs, and so we moved onto the Merrion Suite, taking the crowd with us, but where the same happened again. Ultimately, we moved to Coconut Grove and once again took the crowd with us, where at its peak we had approximately 800 dancers over the two-floor venue. Downbeat ran for over four years and launched the careers of the incredibly talented George and Kevin, who called themselves Nightmares On Wax. The two eventually went their separate ways, and George now lives in Ibiza and has successfully produced over eight albums under the Nightmares On Wax name and is big on the trip-hop scene. Kev, one of the most incredible mixers I have ever seen and who helped me out of numerous tipsy and embarrassing DJ cueing and technical faux pas, remains a successful DJ to this day. We had an incredible time and too many wild nights to mention; there's another book in there somewhere.

I spent my share of the money on records and drunken debauchery and squandered the rest.

On an amusing note, Oky recently confessed he felt I was a traitor during this period, with my furry Kangol, puffa jacket and high tops. I assured him that at the same time I was dancing to House and Hip-Hop, I was DJing Soul and Funk and also buying all the Kent compilations along with contemporary Soul albums, along with playing my Northern collection to anyone who would listen when they came round to the flat. As a result, he has forgiven me, but he's still not feelin the Hip-Hop.

This scene kept us dancing for a decade, but eventually House and Hip-Hop lost their Soul. By this time, I had moved to Manchester, at the time of Richard Searling and Dean Johnson's Parker's nights, Sunset Radio with Mike Shaft, and Alex Lowe's weekenders in Fleetwood, all of which helped me settle in and feel at home. After only a year in Manchester, I was asked to relocate to Holland for work, only to return some four and a half years later. Although there was some Soul in Holland, when I got back to the UK, I was desperate to pick up where I'd left off, but unfortunately all my old mates had hung up their dancing shoes, and so I started going to Blackburn King Georges Hall nights on my own, with its multiple rooms of Northern, Jazz Funk and Modern Soul. Eventually I managed to drag them all off their settees and get back on it at places like Blackburn, Alex's weekenders at Southport, followed later by TSOP at Prestwich and many, many more. I have never stopped dancing through the ages, and particularly enjoyed venues that had Northern rooms, where we could enjoy an hour or two of nostalgia for a genre we had never stopped loving, but then move into another more contemporary room.

Out of the blue, about seven years ago now, Cooky called me up and told me the Central was holding a reunion. I thought that sounded fun, so we made our arrangements to meet up and I put on some soulful threads and leather-soled loafers and made my way to Manchester station to catch the train to Leeds. On arriving, I was on my way to the Adelphi to meet Cooky and Dave, when I heard a voice: "Is that Steve?" I looked round to see Michelle Dudhill and some of her mates. Quite how she recognised me after all these years, I'll never know. It was a bright sunny day, and we ended up having a few pints outside the Adelphi before making our way down to the Central. When I got in, going from the light to the dark, I couldn't see a bloody thing and was literally staggering around bumping into people, many of whom were greeting me, but I genuinely couldn't establish who they were. They must have thought I'd gone blind, or maybe blind drunk. Pretty embarrassing and not quite the reunion I'd imagined.

The blindness passed, and I ended up having a fabulous time, singing along to all the old tunes, reliving the memories, soaking up the atmosphere of the place and meeting many long-lost friends. I attend at least twice a year, and particularly enjoy the annual Christmas piss up, preloading in the Whitelocks before dancing the afternoon away and ultimately jumping on my lonely train home to the wrong side of the Pennines.

Steve Luigi has done a fabulous job of getting us all back together, and we all owe him a debt of gratitude, but now faces the equally challenging job of keeping us all engaged and augmenting us with younger, fitter players, in case we ever hang up our dancing shoes for good.

CHAPTER 10

EPILOGUE

This has been a fantastic experience for me, recalling distant memories, talking to old friends and making new ones.

There were many contributing factors to the formation of the Central as a Soul club in those early years. The mod scene at the cafes, the Blue Gardenia (Bee-Gee) owned by Salvo Dammone, followed by the Conque D'Or (Conk), which on change of ownership became Lulu's, the home of those who literally fought for the Central and were instrumental in its inception as a fully fledged Soul club. The influence of the main precursory Soul club in the city, the Spinning Disc, and its DJs, including Rick Vaughen, Tony Banks and later Hunter Smith. These early venues and many of the people who frequented them merged together to create the foundations for the Central, which ran for more than a decade first time around.

It has uncovered the Central's rich history, from the original nights of mixed modern Beat music through the mod takeover and ultimately the transformation into Northern Soul nights, all in the days before I'd heard of the place. The forceful displacement of the rockers and making the club their own, and then influencing the DJs to play the music they loved from the Wheel and other venues; it's the stuff of urban legend.

A common set of characters emerges from those early days, people such as Pete Dillon, Dave Maltas, Chris Mallows, Denis Billingham, Mike Eastwood and Keith Atkinson, who all played a massive role in making the club what it became for us all over the years. If it hadn't been for them, there might not have been a Soul scene in Leeds, and who knows what paths we might have taken.

There was clearly a period after the Wheel closed and just as the Torch was starting its all-nighters, that Leeds Central became the place to be on the scene. It attracted people from far and wide, and when the Torch eventually closed the Central all-nighters (albeit for only a few months until they were raided and stopped) and just before the all-nighters started in Wigan, attracted all the top names from the world of Northern Soul: Richard Searling DJing, Martyn Ellis and Ian Levine visiting, and Dave Godin intending to go down there, only to get waylaid at Pete Dillon's party.

The night the club was raided will go down in history as one of the most infamous on the Northern scene, and led to the closure of the all-nighters, much the same as happened indirectly at the Wheel and Torch, although in the Central's case, the club was allowed to continue within normal hours. The site of 70 people being arrested and hauled off must have been one to behold, ending a peaceful fun night in Leeds, and displacing its crowds to do pretty much the same thing later in the year at Wigan Casino, albeit on a larger scale. A few had lucky escapes in missing the night, but one or two are still suffering the repercussions some 47 years later.

The evolution of the Central DJs, particularly in those formative Soul years, was fast and fluid, starting with Andy Harrison, with some of the lads who were going to the Wheel influencing him and lending him tunes, Denis Billingham (until he set up Hernie's) the first proper Uptown Soul DJ, followed by resident Northern DJ Keith Atkinson, quickly to be joined by Tony Jackson. Shortly after there was the arrival of local celebrity DJ Tony Banks, hired clandestinely by Joan to bring in the rarer tunes others didn't have.

Tony Banks, who was some 10 years older than the other Central DJs and seemed to have kept himself to himself, did his spot and left. At the time, he was a prolific DJ around West Yorkshire, originally at the various Meccas, but then just about at every club that played any Soul at that time, the Intime, Bali Hi, Hernando's, String of Beads and many more. Listening to him on Richard Searling's Jazz FM show, he had a tone and style of DJing and banter that was reminiscent of famous Radio One DJs of the time, with what may now seem corny links between tracks, but that were absolutely flavour of the day back then. He had an encyclopaedic recollection of artists, venues and labels, and based on his time with Mecca, was given almost every Soul demo on British labels free of charge, particularly Sue, Columbia, Stateside and Tamla Motown; only the BBC were given the equivalent. He built an amazing collection, filling a large bedroom at his house from floor to ceiling, with records that didn't make the grade for him stored in the attic. He later augmented his collection with 15 crates full of US imports he acquired on a trip there in '73, and often when tunes were mentioned, he'd pull out a British demo, British normal copy and American import! Based on stories captured in this book from those who knew him, he was clearly a character and perhaps a little eccentric, with his long frizzy ginger hair and combover, baseball cap and love of all things American, who slept most of the day and talked most of the night, either in person to those who visited his house or over the phone, educating the listener about the music he loved and obsessed with. A sad and major loss to the scene when he passed away, and to cap off the tragedy, all of his amazing collection was practically given away through an auction house, his wife needing the money to put central heating in and oblivious to the fortune they were worth.

During this period of the all-nighters, other celebrity DJs were invited, Richard Searling being the best known and who had built his fame at VaVa's in Bolton. Eventually Keith and Tony J's situation changed when they met their partners to be or moved onto other aspects of their lives, and they hung up their headphones, to be succeeded by Twink and Frank and ultimately joined by Paul Rowan, Steve Luigi, Swish and Fred Ward. As the Northern nights reached their end, Frank was joined by his old friend Paul Schofield to run a new Jazz Funk night on the Fridays. Sometime later the two decided there was still demand for a Northern night and added a Saturday night, bringing in Pat Brady to work with Paul. What is clear is that at every phase of its development, the Central had at least one major headline DJ, someone with their finger on the pulse, who had all the top tunes of the day and constantly broke new ones.

As the Central developed in my era of '74 onwards, we really were spoilt for music. We had the benefit of hearing all of the old Wheel and Torch tunes, and at the same time all of the Mecca and Wigan sounds, but in addition, soulful disco tunes discovered and played by Frank. Later came all the rarities from Paul and Pat, but again coupled with brand-new releases. I don't think there were any other Northern clubs at the time, perhaps with the exception of the Ritz Manchester, that could boast such an eclectic mix of soulful dance music.

Towards the end of the '70s, we had the Jazz Funk era, with Ian and Paul once again putting the Central on Britain's black music map, playing the freshest tunes of the genre often before other clubs, with dancers coming from all over the country to party at the north's hottest club, in both respects.

I am reminded of the great times I had, the scrapes and lucky escapes, the friends I made and the incredible Soul music I heard, over the six or seven years I attended the club on a weekly basis, witnessing its transformation from Northern Soul, through Jazz Funk and ultimately back to Northern again.

The commonality of how most of us were introduced to Northern Soul and discovered the Central, initially hearing the music at youth clubs and smaller venues, avidly reading about it in *Blues & Soul*, trying to track down records in Jumbo and learning from their older customers, and then finally making our way down to the Central where we met likeminded devotees, ultimately to be accepted as part of the scene.

The importance of Jumbo, with Hunter, Lornette and Trevor supplying our records, first from the balcony in the Queens Arcade, then moving to the Merrion Centre and ultimately to the St Johns Centre. Hunter becoming a Mecca DJ, and the shop became a meeting place and supplier of 45s for the Northern Soul crowd, particularly on Saturday afternoons. I thoroughly enjoyed hearing Hunter's story, an important part of the Leeds Soul jigsaw. I bumped into Lornette at a recent event in Chapel Allerton run by Steve Walwyn, himself an old Wigan attendee, and had a good chat with her, letting her know she had supplied a good proportion of my collection and half of Leeds for that matter, which made her smile.

The Central became the centre of our lives, with everything revolving around the club and the comradery of its attendees, living for the weekend and many escaping the monotony of dead-end jobs. Northern Soul and the Central truly were a way of life, a cliché stemming from truth. On the scene we were special, and different from the divs to be found in most towns and cities, whose idea of a night out was getting pissed up and brawling. They were oblivious to the cool subterranean world that was literally happening beneath their feet.

The story from Steve Luigi about resurrecting the Central Soul club with the Sunday all-dayers was emotional, about the impact bullying had on his early years and how he battled that adversity to succeed in life as a Northern DJ, record shop owner, house DJ, and ultimately the man who brought it all back to us. Steve is rightly proud of himself, as I'm sure we are all proud of him for his achievements. We owe him a debt of gratitude.

The experience also brought back some sad memories of racist door policies that were commonplace in the '70s and '80s, some of which persist to this day. Some were overtly racist, but as a lifelong hat wearer, even in the days when I had hair, I remain convinced the "no hat" policies in many clubs was one of the subtler racist door policies, stemming from the fact a disproportionate number of black people like to wear hats. Banning hats and insisting on their removal was aggravating to say the least and still goes on to this day. It's a hat, for fuck's sake, not a lethal weapon, unless of course you're Oddjob! Contrast this with the lack of doormen at the Central and the "anything goes" dress code, as long as you were into the music.

I don't know if it's because I'm older and a bit more sensitive, but as I look back and relive the stories, there seems to have been a lot of violence in those days, and unlike most Soul clubs, some of it was actually inside ours. It makes me smile when I hear people talk about the violence of today and how terrible it is, and I think to myself it wasn't all peace and love back in my day either, and at least I no longer see hundreds of marauding football fans terrorising the city centres. I think the main reason there was violence inside the Central was its location in the centre of a major city, as opposed to more remote Northern Soul venues which you specifically had to travel to, and without a bouncer, it was too easy for drunks to wander in and cause trouble. We policed the club ourselves and they never came back a second time.

I am also saddened by recalling that one or two Soul fans were and probably still are racist, perhaps deluded remnants from skinhead days, the irony escaping them that original skinheads modelled themselves on Jamaican Rude Boys, danced to Soul and Reggae and some were themselves black. This seems all the more perverse when the whole scene is founded on music made by young, gifted and black Americans, as an outpouring against, and a reaction to, the persecution, discrimination and hardship they encountered. Only those few racists themselves know what inadequacies and bitter life experience has made them so hateful.

To massively outweigh this, I enjoyed hearing stories of shared experiences, such as the excitement we all felt on our first trips to the Central and the comradery and pride of feeling we were part of something special, something the divs out there were oblivious to and would never understand anyway. The empathy we felt for black America perhaps relating to the discrimination and drudgery some faced in their own lives, although I'm not sure we would have recognised it as such at the time. Years later, I took a friend of mine, a Soul fan but who was never on the Northern scene, to TSOP in Prestwich, a wonderful two-room event with Northern in one and Modern the other. We stood in the Northern room and as he surveyed the crowd and soaked up the atmosphere, and he turned to me and said, "Well, one thing you can say about this Northern Soul scene is it is working class." I had never really thought about that before, but I think regardless of our socio-economic group, we were and remain the cream of the crop.

We all remember the fashions of the day, and whether we acknowledge it or not what an integral part they played in our peacocking, proudly displaying our clothes for all to see, plus the practicality of having wide trousers and flowing skirts (rarely worn together on the same night) that left our dancing unrestrained.

Dressing up with sophistication and style has always been part of black culture, perhaps stemming back to dressing up for church in the days when religion was more prevalent, and it was one of the few places the black community could come together without fear or harassment. The Soul scene in all its forms is part of this culture. Looking the part goes hand in hand with dancing and the music. To this day I still wear loafers and brogues, selvedge jeans, Oxford button-down shirts, cardigans, Smedley polos, parkas, sheepskin-style pea coats, trilbies and baker boy hats. They all have a modern twist and price tag to match from the designers of the day, but the style reverts back to the clothes of my youth I wore through the seventies. I went to see a psychiatrist recently and he asked me, "How was your childhood?" "It's been alright so far," I replied.

The recollection of how strong the amphetamine drug culture was on the scene, fuelling the all-night dancing and coupled with the criminality of some of those supplying the drugs and to a lesser extent those taking them. Not everyone took drugs, but a large proportion did, and everyone on the scene was exposed to them.

For a handful, the gear became more important than the music and took over their lives, but for the majority it was recreational and went hand in hand with staying awake all night and dancing to the music they loved, albeit with a heightened sense of awareness and a bit of a buzz.

Personally, Northern Soul was the start of a journey into black music, something I have collected, obsessed with and perhaps most importantly danced to my whole life. From Northern to Funk and Jazz Funk, Disco, House and Hip-Hop, but the music and the clubs from those early years and in particular the Central hold a very special place in my heart. I heard a fabulous definition of Soul music recently: "The slow stuff makes you wanna cry and the fast stuff makes you wanna dance." That summarises the sentiment far better than I ever could. It amazes me that some Northern Soul fans can't relate to and will even tell you they don't like Modern Soul (50-year-old Soul) or Soulful House (40-year-old Soul) or, god forbid, contemporary Soul! How can a Soul fan of any period not relate to the likes of Angie Stone, Jill Scott, Mary J Blige, Maysa, Ledisi (Larry Saunders's daughter), Syleena Johnson (Syl's daughter), La La Hathaway (Donny's daughter), Jaheem, Leela James, Kindred Family Soul, Rahsaan Patterson or Anthony Hamilton? It takes all sorts, I suppose, but all that has changed for me is the beat, the music still gives me goosebumps, moves my feet and touches my heart.

We have a common history that bonds us together. Within minutes of meeting people back in the day and the new people I've met writing this, we were sharing stories and experiences, mainly about records, artists and venues that meant so much to us. It feels to me like we are part of a Soul family, and just like families we have disagreements: oldies v newies, Funk versus Northern, white 4x4 beat pop versus slower Soul, Soul versus Disco Soul, Northern versus Modern, who had the best club, who were the best DJs, who were the coolest crowd, who were the best dancers, what was the best time, original vinyl versus bootlegs and digital, and perhaps most importantly the future of the scene. The Northern scene is about danceable Soul music to me and a feeling we are part of something a little exclusive and very special. It is about meeting likeminded people who share our passion for the Soul music, people from all walks of life, parts of the country and backgrounds, none of which matters; we truly are one.

Like many these days, I love collecting vinyl and the thrill of finding a rarity, but at the same time am conscious that many of the people who made the music didn't get paid or receive the recognition they deserved, and that the inflated prices I am paying for rare vinyl never reaches the artist. For that reason, I also buy the tracks on CD, and perhaps we should be promoting CDs and legitimate new reissues (never bootlegs) much more, rather than the inflationary "original vinyl only", to ensure the remaining artists get a slice of the action. Original vinyl doesn't always mean quality in either sound or content, and as Tony Banks said, "It's what's in the grooves that counts."

I know its demand-led, but the prices are climbing out of control, driven by the global popularity of the music and the accessibility on dealer sites and auctions, by people of my generation with disposable income reliving their youth, or everyone wanting to be a DJ these days and play the top 500. Sadly, when we all start dying off, there is a risk our collections end up in clearance sales much as Tony Banks's did all those years ago, and then the bull market will turn to bear. The best strategy is to be last man or woman standing, then you'll clean up! I wish you all long and happy lives and the best of luck.

I remember an event at Prestwich about a decade ago when Alexander Patton performed live. He came on stage, this oldish man with his wife in the wings. He looked at us and sang his heart out, and we reciprocated with our cheers and by following his every word. I had tears in my eyes then, as indeed I have now as I relive the memory. His wife took more pictures of the crowd to show the folks back home than we probably did of him. I am making assumptions about Alexander's life, but judging by his reaction, he had cut a few tunes in the 60s and then gone back to whatever he was doing before to make a living, oblivious to the fact that thousands of miles across the Atlantic he was being hero-worshipped and his records were highly desirable and filling the dancefloors. What is it that bonds Northern Soul artist and fan? It's obviously the love of Soul music, but I've also got to believe it's the empathy that a shared life experience of struggle brings, theirs much more than most of ours.

The Central has gone through phases, and it will be interesting to see the next one develop. The reunions have been fantastic, a lot of fun and have worked well, but I can't help thinking there is a risk of them becoming a parody of the early days, with a dwindling group of attendees constantly trying to relive their youth by listening to the same old music, with some even dressing the way we did in the 70s, not a great look when you're in your 60s complete with bald heads and pot bellies. It hasn't happened, but if it did it would be a travesty for one of the longest running Soul clubs in Britain.

For me, the Northern scene was a continuation of the modernist culture of my predecessors, always forward-looking and cutting edge. That's not entirely possible when the core of the music we love is over 50 years old, but there are more recent untapped veins of Soul dance music that could still be referred to as Northern Soul, whatever that might be. Northern is obviously a genre we Brits made up and doesn't exist to the creators of the music itself, which they cut as R&B, up-tempo Soul, Disco, Funk and even Jazz. With that inclusive and progressive philosophy, why can't up-tempo contemporary Soul and Soulful House be played on the scene all in the same room, after all, it is mature enough now, and some of it is rare and highly collectable and its great soulful dance music? Who is the DJ big and brave enough to take us on that journey, blending the old with the new and attracting a younger crowd to re-energise us and keep us on our toes, securing the future of the scene for decades to come? We might have a little moan along the way about it not being proper Northern, much as some of the older crowd did when the Mecca disco tunes were introduced, but eventually we'll accept them, and who knows, may grow to love them. We should not only keep the faith but spread it so our successors can enjoy the same incredible experience we have and provide a home for our much-cherished vinyl when it's finally over for us and we're on our way.

The book lists hundreds of tunes, the ones that hold a special place in the hearts of those who contributed. I'm guessing you'll know most of them, but hopefully there are some you don't, and you'll track them down on Spotify, YouTube and vinyl or CD. There are also perhaps a hundred or so people mentioned, a significant proportion of those who attended. If you are not included, I apologise for the omission. I did try and follow up when people said, "You must talk to so and so," but had to draw the line somewhere, otherwise there was a chance I wouldn't complete the book in my lifetime. Hopefully you'll recognise someone who is included and empathise with their recollection, and if you bend my ear sufficiently, I'll try and include you in any reprints.

The Central started its modern life as a multicultural mod dance club, playing Soul and a little Ska and Reggae. It then slowly transformed into a Northern Soul club, and many black people drifted away to pursue the newly emerging Funk sound at Primo's. The outside world became increasingly divided and racist with the emergence of the NF, and the black crowd had to avoid these violent thugs as they made their way through town and down to the clubs. Sadly, one or two people associated with the Northern scene flirted with far-right groups, while the vast majority were true Soul brothers and sisters. The Central then reunited likeminded black, white and all ethnicities around Jazz, Funk and ultimately back to Soul. To capture this multicultural sentiment, I have taken the liberty of slightly modifying our badge, as you can see from the front cover. An incredible social journey centred around an incredible club, a journey that has massively influenced my life and contributed to who I am today, and one we can all rightly feel proud to have been part of.

Oky, Maureen, me and Dave at a reunion

Cooky, my brother Andy, me, Dave and Oky at a reunion